Is There Fun After Paul?

A Theology of Clowning
By Mark Liebenow

Resource Publications, Inc.
160 E. Virginia St. No. 290
San Jose, CA 95126

Editorial Director: Kenneth Guentert
Cover Design: Christine Benjamin
Production Editor: Scott Alkire
Pasteup Artists: Geoff Rogers, Ron Niewald

ISBN 0-89390-066-4
Library of Congress Catalog Number: 86-60890
Printed and Bound in the United States 5 4 3 2 1

Contents

Illustrations _____

Acknowledgments

The author wishes to thank the authors and publishers who have given permission to use material from their publications

Abingdon Press for *Hammer of the Lord*, by Colin Morris, 1973; Doug Adams for *Humor in the American Pulpit*, the Sharing Company, 1975, "In Forming Liturgies With Parables" from *Modern Liturgy*, May 1981, "Bringing Biblical Humor to Life in Liturgy," *Modern Liturgy*, Dec/Jan 1979, and from his "Humor and Faith" class at the Pacific School of Religion; *Anglical Theological Review* for "The Priestly Fool," by Ken Feit; *Aramco World Magazine* for "Bring on the Clowns"; *The Atlantic Monthly* for "The Use of Comic Spirit in Religion," copyright c 1911 by William Austin Smith as first published in the Atlantic Monthly, reprinted with permission; J. Martin Bailey for "Here Come God's Clowns," *AD 1982* Magazine, February 1982, and for the use of his pictures; Richard S. Bernardo for "A Serious Meditation on Laughter* (*or, As I Lay Laughing),"*Evangelion* , Fall 1981; Kevin M. Bradt for "Body Language Centers of Energy in Keaton and Chaplin;" Margie Brown for "Clowning for the Cops," "What Clowns Always Wanted to Know About Sex," "Taboo or Not Taboo," and "Clowning Du Jour" from *Modern Liturgy*, August 1981; *Calliope Magazine* for Tom Niccolls "Praise of Faith" columns, March 1979; Robert McAfee Brown for his forward; The Christian Science Publishing Society for "Laughter is a Serious Subject," by Robert Nye, September 30, 1975 issue of the *Christian Science Monitor*, Columbia University Press for *Fools and Folly During the Middle Ages and the Renaissance*, by Barbara Swain, © 1932, reprinted with permission; Don Dewey for his drawing of the nose-glasses; Patricia deJong for her unpublished thesis, "Improvisation: The Art of Relationship;" Excerpt from *Clowning in Rome* by Henri J.M. Nouwen, copyright © 1979 by Henri J.M. Nouwen, reprinted by permission of Doubleday and Co, Inc.; Excerpt from *Portrait of Karl Barth* by George Casalis, copyright © 1963 by Doubleday and Company, Inc, reprinted by permission of Doubleday and Company, Inc; Harper and Row for permission to use material from *Wishful Thinking* by Frederick Buechner, *The Prophets: An Introduction* by Abraham Heschel, *Message of the Prophets* by Gerhard von Rad, *The Humor of Christ* by Elton Trueblood, *Raid on the Articulate* by John Dominic Crossan, *In Parables* by John Dominic Crossan; Indiana University Press for *Circus and Culture: A Semiotic Approach*, by Paul Bouissae; Harvard University Press for *The Feast of Fools* by Harvey Cox, © 1969; Bobbie Hineline for her unpublished parable; Tim Kehl for his "Theology of Clowning," in *Shoddy Pad*, 1978 and *Modern Liturgy*, August 1981, "Clown Message, Christian Message;" "The Healing Magic of Clowns," by Susan Ambrose, reprinted from *Kiwanis* magazine, copyright 1969 by Kiwanis International; McGraw-Hill Book Company for *The Joys of Yiddish* by Leo Rosten, 1968, reproduced with permission; J.C. McLelland for his *The Clown and the Crocodile*, John Knox Press, 1970; Webster's Third New International Dictionary for their definitions of fun and fool, © 1981 by Mirriam-Webster Inc, publishers of the Mirriam-Webster Dictionaries: *Military Chaplain's Review* for "The Clown, Another Fool for Christ's Sake," by Floyd Shaffer; Minneapolis Star and Tribune for "The World's Smallest Circus" by Robert T. Smith, March

19, 1980; Mowbray's Publishing Division, Oxford, for *Barnabas* by Graham Jeffery; London Management and Stewart Parker for *Spokesong*; Michael Moynahan for his "Mime and Worship," 1981 *Shoddy Pad*, and from *Modern Liturgy*, "Discovering God's Gift of Humor Through Liturgical Mime," "Discovering the Experience of Sacrament Through Mime," and "Proclamation;" *National Catholic Reporter* for "Compassionate Clown," August 28, 1981; Thomas Merton: *New Seeds of Contemplation*, copyright © 1961 by The Abbey of Gethsemani, Inc, reprinted by permission of New Directions Publishing Corporation; Thomas Merton: *The Wisdom of the Desert*, copyright © 1960 by The Abbey of Gethsemani, Inc, reprinted by permission of New Directions Publishing Corporation; Jubilee for "God Loves Clowns" by Floyd Shaffer, December 1979 issue of *The Other Side*; Oxford University Press for *Perfect Fools: Folly for Christ's Sake in Catholic and Orthodox Spirituality* by John Saward, 1980; the following material which first appeared in *Parabola Magazine*, Vol. IV, No. 1, "One More Smile for a Hopi Clown" by Emory Sekaquaptewa, and "The Wisdom of the Contrary: A Conversation with Joseph Epes Brown" by D.M. Dooling; Pilgrim Press for *The Comic Vision* by Conrad Hyers, 1981; *The Priest* for "Liturgy and Imagination: The Next Phase of Renewal?" by Patrick Collins, November 1979; Princeton University Press for *Fictional Transfigurations of Jesus* by Theodore Ziolkowski, copyright 1972, excerpt; Random House for *Souls on Fire: Portraits and Legends of Hasidic Masters*, by Elie Wiesel, © 1972; Shocken Publishers for *Tales of the Hasidim: The Early Masters*, by Martin Buber, 1947; Leo Remington for his quote about happy havoc; Floyd Shaffer for "Fools for Christ, Clowns for Christ," "Faith and Fantasy" on Thesis Theo. Cassettes, and ideas; Simon and Schuster for *Zorba the Greek*, by Nikos Kazantzakis, 1952; Thesis for "Faith and Fantasy" cassette by Floyd Shaffer; John Towsen for his book *Clowns*, 1976, E.P. Ditton; Univ. of Notre Dame Press for *Elie Wiesel: Messenger to all Humanity*, by Robert McAfee Brown, 1983; Westminster Press for *Christ in a Pluralistic Age* by John Cobb, 1975; Mark Wiley for "His Offering," from *alive now!* M/A 1979 © 1979 by the Upper Room; Adapted from *The Alphabet of Grace* by Frederick Buechner, copyright © 1970 Frederick Buechner, published by Winston/Seabury Press (formerly published by the Seabury Press), 430 Oak Grove, Minneapolis, MN 55403, all rights reserved, used with permission; Hilda Petri of the John G. Neihardt Trust for *Black Elk Speaks* by John G. Neihardt, Pocket Books, 1972; Tom Woodward for material from a conversation; John Wallace on his unpublished article on street clowning; Rick Bernardo and Cindy Winton-Henry for allowing me to observe them improvising; respectively, on the piano and dancing; and to Randall Mullins, Christoph Huss, Linda McFadden, Don Dewey, Evelyn MacNair, and Nancy Hall for their help and talents with regards to drawings and pictures.

At the time of this writing, I have been unable to locate Beverly and Emmett Kelley who hold the rights to *Clown*, by Emmett Kelley, Prentice-Hall, 1954; Julia Williams and Stephen Greiner for their article, "Therapeutic Clowning as a Treatment Modality;" Patrick Forbes for "Gospel Fool;" the copyright holder for Hiler Harzberg and Arthur Moss's book, *Slapstick and Dumbbell*, Joseph Lawren, publisher, 1924; and the authors of "Charlie," from *Arts in Context*, June 1978, and "The Clown Pledge of Allegiance." Credit will be given in future editions if the information has been found.

Foreword

by Robert McAfee Brown

Something crazy is going on. A man named Job takes God to account for wrecking his life, and God invites him to contemplate the hippopotamous.

A man named Joshua (or, as we have come to say, Jesus), searching for an apt simile, suggests that the chances of a rich man making it into the Kingdom of Heaven are about equal to the chances of a camel squeezing through the eye of the needle. A real gas. Unless you happen to be a rich man.

It's not just the occasional episodes in the overall story that are so wild. It is the very structure of the story itself. Get this: the story tells us that there is a God on the scene, a God powerful enough to have made up the whole scene, from the props to the spotlights to the grease paint, and also who happens to have constructed the plot that is being enacted. And this mighty Author-Designer decides to make an appearance on stage, right in the middle of the story.

So where does the Author-Designer appear, with all that power to tap? In one of the early scenes, people are looking in the midst of earthquakes, wind and fire — great backdrops for displays of power such as the Author-Designer clearly possesses.

But that's all a ruse. For where is the thundering majesty finally located? In "a still, small voice," the least likely place of all. Power in the very absence of power. Capricious, if not downright irresponsible, for God to lead people astray like that . . .

And then, in a later scene, when the story has been fleshed out some more, and a personal appearance of the Author-Designer in the form of a King is definitely in the cards, the hand that gets dealt is a real surprise, dominated by the joker, for the King who comes is not actually a "king" at all, but a defenseless baby, whose parents live on the wrong side of the tracks, and whose only "throne" turns out to be a cross bar on a dump heap, where he is abandoned to die with a couple of convicted criminals.

Not exactly the stuff of belly laughs, but *so far off the mark from what we would have expected*, or would have scripted ourselves if we had taken pen to hand, that we find ourselves having to take second and third looks, asking over and over again, "*What* is going on here?"

And that's where the clowns come in. For clowns don't do things the way we would either. Clowns throw us off balance. Clowns force us to reflect, "Well if *that's* the way things are, maybe . . ." Maybe, almost anything: maybe the world is different from what we expected, maybe we have to be ready for surprises, maybe God has a sense of humor, maybe bulbous noses and wild purple wigs are better clues to human nature than dour faces and properly groomed hair.

In the pages that follow, Mark Liebenow has captured something of the world of a clown, and shown how the clown can even be . . . a messenger of God. That's not only the last thing in the world one would expect from a "religious book." It's also the last thing in the world one would expect in an "academic dissertation," which is what these pages technically were, once upon a time. In fact, I'd be willing to bet that the oral examination on the academic dissertation was fun (a first in *academe*), and that the examiners all wore face masks to make them look like Groucho Marx. But don't take me up on the wager. You'll lose and I'll win. For I was there. Behind one of the masks.

Prologue

Why am I concerned about clowning, especially about a theology of clowning? Simply put, I need it. If my friends didn't drag me off on adventures from time to time, I would think all the time and celebrate very little. I know I need to be more of a clown.

A clown lives life. I stay in my house and plan how to live it. A clown accepts chaos as the normal living situation. I try to put everything in order before venturing forth to do something creative. Of course, I never reach my goal of complete order before my paper construction comes tumbling down around me. When a clown wants to do something, the clown does it, right then and there. When I get a notion, I check my schedule to see if I can afford to fit it in. I love a clean desk. I suspect a clown delights in having a desk so messy that papers and books are sliding into the floor.

I realize that not enough of what I do is spontaneous. Not enough is done for the pure pleasure or delight of it. Not enough is done because I feel God wants me to do it, even though I'd rather do something else, like complete another project. For me, the pleasure of work easily slides into the need to work in order to feel affirmed and secure. I want to be open to what is here today, in this hour, in this place, and with the people who are around me now. I suspect my salvation is tied in with just how well I learn to play.

When I put on whiteface, I feel transformed. The presence of even this thin mask makes it much easier for me to be who I want to be. I am less inhibited. I can play with certain behaviors to see how they feel, and keep them if they fit. A clown is free to try anything. By borrowing some of this freedom, I find myself responding more to who I am and less to what other people think I should be. I wear a smile and a tear as a part of my clown face to remind myself of the clown's involvement with all the emotions and needs of life.

As I learn to be a better clown, my ability to live in chaos will keep me on the growing edges of life. This is the area of marginality, the place where the present is being lived and the future is forming. I will be saved by laughter, or not be saved at all. This I believe with all my foolish heart.

This book is not the usual work done on clowning that tells you how to put on make-up, or gives you set skits to perform for different occasions. This book aims to help you understand what clowning is about and discover how to let your clown out. It aims at the foundation of clowning, its grounding in reality, so that you can gather together with other clowns and create your own skits, ones that address your needs and local situation better than mass-produced skits can do. In the way of an old saying, I would rather teach you how to clown forever, than to give you a couple of clown skits to last this weekend. Clowning, if it is to reach out and touch people, must come out of your heart and out of your soul. If it is to be transforming, it must be rooted in humility, love, joy, and a profound sense of celebration for all creation.

It has been a real circus doing this book. I hope it is also a circus to read. (I wonder who's going to play the lead in the movie version.)

A smiling box
is often mistaken
for something
it is not.
But then,
what isn't?

Dedication

To Ken Feits and Nick Weber
two fools

Steve Cary and Evelyn McNair
two clowns peopling around in the Moravian Church

and to

Patricia deJong
who helps me see life as one big improv

my gratitude goes to
Doug Adams, Robert McAfee Brown, and Michael Moynahan
who guided me in my writing

and to the people of the Graduate Theological Union Library
who helped me with the research

CHAPTER 1
God's Love of Laughter

> My eyes were watering. An agonizing ache left my stomach in knots . . . I thought I would die. I found the courage to attempt a gulp of air — "I may be fine after all," it dawned on me. Head clearing and eyes drying, I picked my racked body off the floor. "Whew. A close one," I sighed. "Has anyone ever really *died* from laughing? . . . God. Oh God what a way to go . . ." And immediately I dropped to the fetal position again, struggling once more against being overcome by this tidal power, this mystic force: laughter. This is serious stuff.
>
> — Rick Bernardo[1]

Some say God created the world out of loneliness. Others say the world was created because the Almighty loves stories. I believe the world was created because God has a sense of humor and adventure. And when creation was completed, God saw that it was good and laughed! Then God rested. Michael Moynahan says the Almighty *had* to rest because of laughing so hard over the whole thing.[2]

God created the world for fun; not as a place for human beings to work through their sins, nor as a place for rewarding the good and punishing the bad. The agony model for Christian life only fits if we stop at the crucifixion. The reality of the resurrection beyond the crucifixion moves the church and Christians into celebration. Too often Christians get hung up on finding the correct beliefs, whether or not they actually believe them, and forget to live those beliefs in their everyday lives.

God loves a good joke, and I believe God loves to laugh more than anything else, although direct references to such are few in the Bible.

> The ancient Hebrews had to know laughter as a friend. You had better be able to laugh at a God who goes by the me "I Am who I Am." Moses is reported to have remarked, "What is this joke?" (Yahweh): "You can call me "I Am" for short. On second thought, don't call me; I'll call you."[3]

If God didn't love to laugh, then why create giraffes and rhinoceroses? Why tease with the wisdom of this world by choosing to work through the simple, the foolish, and the powerless as God has done so often? Why choose Moses to be the speaker for the Israelites when Moses stumbled over his tongue? Why make the Israelites the "Chosen People" when they lived in the geographical doormat of the Middle East? And why choose a wishy-washy person like Peter, give him a name that means "Rock," and say, "Upon this wishy-washy person I will build my church?" Who is God kidding? Who is going to believe and trust in a God like this? Who indeed, except that God must have a profoundly deep sense of humor. It just doesn't make sense otherwise.

The most authentic response we can give to this humorous God is deep laughter. I am not talking about polite little sniffles that are hidden behind embroidered hankies and tweed coatsleeves. I am talking about the rumbling that knocks around inside one's guts for a while before exploding out the throat with a hearty, resounding shout of delight! I mean the kind of event that makes young people faint and old people lose their dentures. This is the way to show appreciation to God. "Rumor has it among linguists and word-doctors," Rick Bernardo reports, "that this word (laughter) derives from the Sanskrit *lokha*, which meant trying to belch while riding on the back of a yak in full flight."[4] There are certainly more ways to worship than to pray God to death.

Laughter is one aspect of human life that is too often missing, too often put down as vulgar and as belonging to the low life. The higher one goes in religious circles, the more reserved and somber one is expected to be. Laughter is a serious subject, and a mysterious one. But it should remain somewhat fun. Rabbi Abraham Heschel said, "To be really alive, to be holy, one needs discipline, artistry, and a little foolishness!" Martin Luther played with humor by using popular beerhall tunes for his religious hymns. His congregations were shocked. Yet through the tunes, Luther touched a depth in his congregations that had not been reached by traditional music. In his 1977 movie, *Annie Hall*, Woody Allen affirmed the importance of laughter after an encounter in bed: "Boy, (sigh) . . . that was the most fun I've had without laughing . . ."

Too seldom is laughter appreciated for its magnificent healing powers. Laughing . . .

> . . . is one of the healthiest things a body can do. Lungs and diaphragm get an excellent workout, as do stomach muscles. Heart muscles are massaged by the motion, and the entire cardiovascular system flourishes and rejoices, circulating the news. Facial muscles experience new-found postures, a kind of visage-yoga . . .[5]

Norman Cousins is convinced that laughter was involved in his recovery from ankylosing spondylitis, a chronic, progressive disease. He chronicles his experience in his book, *Anatomy of an Illness*. As a major part of this treatment, he watched hundreds of films of the great masters of comedy, and literally laughed himself to health.

Humor, and its response, laughter, are also emptying. This aspect is needed in church, because we are often too full of schedules and time-tables to let the Word of God in. And in this world of increasing concern about efficiency and the ability to mass-produce, laughter is one of the last remaining worthless, untaxable, individual activities left.

There are many styles of laughter to express shades of reactions. Bernardo writes, "I knew a woman in college who sounded like a dying whooping crane when she laughed; certain people lived their lunch times in terror of that laugh. Some of us bark like dogs; others more like seals. Some whinny like a horse. Some do angry sea-gull impressions."[6] When I'm really tickled, I sound like a donkey choking on food.

Humor is one of the most humanizing gifts we have. It helps us celebrate the contradictions of life and of who we are.[7] By laughing at ourselves when we are foolish, we accept the reality of being part-hero and part-fool; part-success and part-failure. We find a sense of balance. Laughter can be both the medium and the message. But above all, it is a starting place for something new. "I believe laughter is sacred," Bernardo confesses. "I believe it is a gift, an infusion of grace from God. I believe laughter participates in God. It's difficult not to love someone when you are laughing with them."[8]

Fools in History

There have always been clowns in the world, although they have not all been costumed as circus clowns are today. There have always been those individuals who dared to bend the given perception of reality in order to reveal new dimensions. Good clowning sets two world crashing against each other. The result may be laughter, awe, shock, or even disorientation. Properly done, however, clowning offers new and better visions to replace the old, and now limiting ones. Clowning offers a way to see the deeper roots of reality.

Through the years those who have tried to introduce these new perceptions have been called clowns, fools, monks, or simply mad. And although each culture has had its clowns, they tend to flourish only among cultures that value symbols and sacraments as well as tools.[9] A lesson is to be learned from the tales of King Arthur. Of all the knights who went out from his court to find the Holy Grail, only one found it. Parsifal. The name means "Perfect Fool."[10]

In many tribal societies the religious leaders double as clowns. They are known in this dual capacity by such names as tricksters, shamans, Koyemshi, and Heyhokas. Tricksters make fun of religious ceremonies to affirm the need for cultural boundaries, and to show the people that their revered leaders are only human.

Shamans are found in the Americas and in Africa, and are

sometimes called witchdoctors. As priest, they administer medicine and function as mediaries between the people's fears and the threatening spirits of nature. They work with such matters as the fears of hunters about to head out to kill game. The appropriate spirits are prayed to in hopes of convincing the spirits to allow a good hunt and to allow everyone to return home safely. Tribal members are assured by the work of the shamans that the tribe has some control over their lives, and are not at the total mercy of the spirits.

The clownish side of shamans comes out when the knowledge of a greater being is mixed with the use of magic to confound rationality, to shock, and to inspire. These are common clown goals, although magic is seldom used by circus clowns. Being able to perform magic indicates that the performer has a highly-developed skill. Clowns never quite have the knack to do anything successfully. The Canadian Dakotas believe the clown is the most powerful of shamans.

One of the North American tribes that has clowns is the Hopi. What follows is a description of how these clowns work:

> The Hopi Indians have a bizarre figure among their rich gallery of Kachi dancers. Among the expected figures representing deities and animal spirits, they have the figure of the Koyemshi, or "Mudheads." These are their clowns. Their purpose is to invade the solemn ceremonies at a certain point, usually launching themselves from the roof of one of the adobe huts. In a manner similar to our Keystone Cops, they stumble over each other and pester the audience and even the sacred dancers. They are permitted and even expected to mock and harass the solemn rituals. One purpose for their antics is simply comic relief for long ceremonies, but a deeper reason is that they gain sacred power for the people by ritually infringing on taboos and literally planning with sacred and solemn ceremonies.[11]

In effect, they are saying, 'Be serious about our religious rites and use them as guides. But do not make idols out of them by taking them too seriously.' The structures that hold the culture together are re-affirmed as necessary by the clown skits, yet the relative *nature* of the structures are made clear. It is not that *these* structures are here, but that *some* structures are. According to Emory Sekaquaptewa, the Hopi feel every person is called to be a clown in his or her daily life.[12]

Sekaquaptewa tells a story that illustrates the Hopi perspective on even the normally serious topic of someone's death. When it came time to die, an old clown made his fil request. He wanted to go out as a clown.

So after he died, he was dressed up in his costume, and taken to the roof of one of the adobe houses by the plaza. The pall-bearers picked his body up and swung it over the plaza. They did this three times; each time as if to throw the body down. Each time they yelled

"Yaahahay!" The fourth time they let go and the body fell down, plop, in the plaza. At first the people gathered to pay their respects were shocked. Then they realized the significance of the event — that not even death could take this man's humor away — and everybody laughed.[13] Not even death is to be taken with a totally straight face.

Joseph Epes Brown has had extensive experience with the tribes of the North American Plains. He says the use of shock is important in tribal clowning for moving people out of their "petty little concerns about the routines of daily life."[14] Then, with the people alert and open, the perception of a reality greater than ordinary life can enter. Humor does this, he suggests, *because* it takes place within a serious religious context.

> It is you might say a shattering of the structure of the rite in order to get at the essence of the rite. It seems to ridicule, thus destroy, but it does this so that the deeper truths contained within the rite can come forth and reveal themselves.[15]

It is this shattering of the expected that gives the clown bite.

Hopi clowns not only work with the essence of the rite, they also try to get at the essence of people. If someone in the tribe is doing something harmful, the clowns will act it out in public, and poke fun at the behavior and at the person.[16] Usually the unwanted behavior quickly ends.

In much the same way, Sioux coyote tales, and Pueblo clowns catch the attention of their people by sexual displays that are normally taboo for their tribe, and which would normally disrupt their patterns of life. They wear false genitals and simulate intercourse. But by portraying such banned actions in public, and in a controlled manner, the people's own desire to do such is released. The skits act as a safety valve.[17]

Plains Heyhokas

The Heyhokas of the Plains Native American culture provide another example of how tribal religious clowns bring about new revelations.

> . . . they do things upside down or backwards; sometimes they will pitch a tepee with the poles on the outside of the lodge covering, with the smoke flags facing the wrong way, or with the doorway to the west instead of to the east . . . Sometimes instead of going in the doorway they lift up the lodge cover at the back and crawl under; things like that . . .
> I like the one Black Elk used to tell about the Heyhokas who rushed out of the tepee after a little sprinkling of rain and saw a large puddle. With great flourishes and gesticulations they took off their clothes down to the breech cloth, and then they got a long pole, about twenty feet long, and laid it horizontal, across the puddle; then they set it up vertically in order to measure the depth of

the water, and saw it was about twenty feet deep, you see? So with a great deal of display, making sure everybody in camp was looking, they dove into the water, which was only a few inches deep, and hit their heads hard, and made everybody laugh. And that's good, because what is life without laughter? It's very important.[18]

Black Elk fulfilled the two roles for the Sioux. He was a religious leader and a clown. The seeming incongruity of being both never bothered him, for the Sioux also recognize the sacredness of humor. Often in the middle of an important religious ceremony, the opening of a medicine bundle, for instance, the participants are expected to tell jokes. Soon everyone is rolling around on the ground.[19]

Native Americans on the Northwest coast are actually prohibited from starting certain ceremonies until the guests have laughed. The conviction is that laughter prepares the ground for opening up to the second dimensions.[20] Brown says this realization of the world of appearances as illusory, "of maya as the Hindus would say," helps people to break through to a deeper reality.[21]

Pu-tai (d. 916), the pot-bellied laughing Buddha, is an example of the fool in Zen Buddhism. Like a warm-weather Santa Claus, he left the security of monastic rule to wander from place to place, laughing and playing with children, and giving them gifts. His vision was an "acceptance of events and objects as they are while at the same time celebrating the inexhaustible significance and mystery in the most commonplace."[22] Ho-tai, the Japanese equivalent of Pu-tai, Hanshan (ca. 627-60), and Ryo-kan Taigu (1758-1831) were also Zen Buddhist fools.

Islamic Sufi fools are found in the dervishes who meditate by "whirling." They also pose riddles designed to lead to enlightenment, like Zen koans and Christian parables. The most famous Sufi fools were Mulla Nasreddin Hoja (b. ca. 1227), and Bohlul.

For all these religious groups, by whatever names their clowns and fools were known, laughter is essential to their way of life. Laughter is a unique tool for opening people's eyes up to something greater than everyday reality.

Circus clowns also have a diversity of functions. The traditional image of the clown as an entertainer of children is accurate and valuable, but it is also limiting. Clowns do more. Rodeo clowns protect rodeo riders from the thrashing animals. Circus clowns, like Emmett Kelly, play with the taboos of society: power, wealth, sexuality, and death, as a way of opening up new perspectives on reality. And movie clowns, like Charlie Chaplin and Buster Keaton, seek to humanize the developing technological society by revealing modern problems in outrageous skits.

Clowns dissolve "facts" back into reality, back to where the breathing, living, feeling reactions that are codified by the facts have no pretension of meaning more than what they are by themselves. All clowns try to point out that no matter how bad life is now, there is always reason to hope for something better in the future.

Christian Clowns

The diversity of functions for religious clowns in the Christian Church continues to develop. *Social Action* clowning plays with and challenges the blindly-held taboos and values of church and society for authenticity. It tries to show people how to see from a third, and more holistic, perspective, rather than to regard any situation as being either right or wrong.

Liturgical clowning seeks to renew the sense of expectation and creativity in the worship and devotional areas of Church life. And like the clowns in other religions, liturgical clowns seek to deepen the congregation's experience through the use of laughter.

Therapeutic clowning tries to reach through the walls of the withdrawn, the lonely, and the broken — and to heal them by visiting them in their homes, in hospitals, and in nursing homes.

Finally, there is *theological* clowning, which is not done in greasepaint. I believe all Christians are called to do theological clowning, for this involves bringing specific attitudes into one's everyday life; attitudes of hope, joy, humility, and love, which are the core of all Christian faith.

As humor without faith can lead to despair, faith without humor can become arrogant and intolerant.[23] The holistic attitude of clowning includes humor and faith as enablers of each other. Over 70 years ago, William Austin Smith said, "Every Divinity School might well have in its senior year, along with courses in systematic divinity, and homiletics, a course in the great masters of comedy."[24]

All Christian clowns have celebration as their major concern. They want to celebrate God's active presence in the daily events of this world, and to affirm the basic goodness of this life. They want to renew the sense of wonder in each human life, that each person may see life from inclusive, not exclusive perspectives. The aim is not to judge people, but to transform people and situations into what is deeper, broader, and more faith-filled. Not everyone is called to put on greasepaint for Christ, as not all are called to be pastors, or teachers, or prophets. But all Christians are called to believe in and live the folly of the cross, and this makes clowns of us all.

The clowns, fools, and tricksters of all societies try to restore the balance of work and play, reverence and irreverence. They want to affirm the need to be serious at times without being solemn; to be respectful without being idolatrous; and to be religious without being judgmental. They do this by re-symbolizing the traditions of the past, so that the old meanings may be experienced with new life.

CHAPTER 2
Fools and Clowns Throughout History

> (about Black Elk, a Sioux) Well, just as a Heyhoka, a sometimes clown figure, he liked to make people laugh; he felt happy when people were laughing. When there were any little children around he would always be doing funny things with them or telling them funny stories, to make them laugh. I think he understood that there is no access to a deeper spiritual reality if there is not the opening force of laughter present there. It tends to open the heart for receiving a greater value than that of this world.
> — Joseph Epes Brown, *Parabola*, Feb. 1979, p. 63

There have always been clowns in the world. The first one may well have been someone who thought he could get a laugh by picking up a bear. The joke was for him when he lost his grip and the bear came crashing down on top. His friends probably had a big laugh over that.[1] The first references to the transforming style of clown laughter exist in religious accounts. In ancient Egypt, where bands of brightly-dressed entertainers cavorted through the streets, they worshiped a god called "Typhon." Some authorities believe this god represents the deification of the clown. Typhon was depicted as having a "huge gross face and a long projecting tongue."[2]

Greece had comedians among its tumblers, jugglers and rope dancers as early as 800 B.C.[3] One report says, "In the time of Aristophanes, the best joke of the clown Hermon was to slam a stick against the skulls of his fellow actors, while the comique Parmenon got laughs by imitating the grunting of a hog."[4] Not very sophisticated humor, but it still works today. This stick was an early form of the court jester's sceptre and the clown's slapstick. All of them are, in a way, phallic symbols. They are used as an extension of male sexuality as a way of playing with the boundaries of each culture's stand on sex. Exaggerated breasts are a common extension of female sexuality.

Rome formalized the Greek comedy situations. In their book, *Slapstick and Dumbbell*, Hiler Harzberg and Arthur Moss write:

> The Romans acquired the clown along with many other refinements of Greek civilization. Buffoons were in high favor with the Romans and brought comic relief to the otherwise dull and heavy banquet . . . These were Maccus with his low flat forehead, monstrous drooping mask, and double hunch on his back . . .; Bucco the jabbering insolent swaggering parasite . . .; Pappus the ridiculous old miser . . .; and Dossenus the knavish soothsayer . . .[5]

In the sixth century, after the fall of Rome, the conquering barbarians closed all theaters, and clowns had to take to the streets to earn a living. Some level-headed thinkers today would probably say the barbarians made a civilized decision.

1000 A.D.

Clowns are never gone very long. They always find a way to sneak back into the picture. Consider the University of Bologna. It was founded in 1088 A.D. and was one of the world's oldest and most respected places of higher learning. Yet, whenever a professor felt the students were growing sleepy or inattentive, a small door would open above the speaker's lectern, and a clown's head would pop out. The clown would tell a few jokes to wake the students up, and then disappear.[6]

The golden age of fools began in the thirteenth century, and included the development of the Christian Feast of Fools. This will be discussed later when Christian clowning is taken up in detail.

In the sixteenth century, as church clowning ended, secular clowning resurged into prominence. Joyful Societies sprang up around France, and the Commedia dell' Arte began in Italy. Both presented situation comedies using set characters. In the Commedia, there were five: the sly Arlechinno, Pantalone, Pulcinello, Pierrot, the sad white-faced character who always lost the beautiful Columbine to Arlechinno. Their names were altered in England to be Harlequin, Pantaloon, Mr. Punch, Pierrot (who became the clown), and Columbine. Some scholars try to show how the Commedia characters descended from Roman drama, but it seems probable that clowns rise spontaneously out of all cultures, and re-invent the old forms of comedy.[7]

Shakespeare

In his plays, Shakespeare used clowns and fools as a link between the stage and the audience. The characters Bottom, from *A Midsummer Night's Dream*, and Dogberry, from *Much Ado About Nothing*, are two examples of his clowns. In the 1590s William Kempe and Richard Cowley generally played these parts, Kempe, in particular, was known for his "broad humor, comic dancing, and frequent ad-libs."[8] When Kempe was replaced by Robert Armin in 1599, fools began to replace clowns in Shakespeare's plays, although fools were not common in Elizabethan drama. The parts of Feste, Touchstone, and King Lear's fool were written for Armin's talents. It seems that the criticism by Hamlet warning clowns "not to speak more than is laid down for them," was directed by Kempe for his habit of ad-libbing away from the lines written down. This play was first performed shortly after his departure.[9]

Another Shakespearean clown is Falstaff, "who enjoys the

richness of creation so much that he lacks time and taste for the orderliness of polite society. He is not only untidy; he is a liar. (Nathan Scott declares that Falstaff lies in order to protect himself against the conventional dishonesty of other men.)"[10] When Prince Hal becomes the respectable Henry V, Falstaff is booted out of Hal's confidence. No longer is his life-affirming clownishness valued.

The Puritans closed the English theaters in 1642. When they reopened in the 1660s, clowns were back on the streets.[11]

Other Cultures

Although there were no clowns in the original Sanskrit epics of India, a great deal of action is given to the clown-servant, Vidusaka, when the epics are performed on stage. Vidusaka is usually paired with Vita, who plays the clever part to Vidusaka's density. This mirrors the pairing of Harlequin with Pierrot, as well as the comedy teams in Chinese and Balinese drama.[12]

Clowns in the Javanese religion are like the Hopi Koyemshi. They are both keepers and disrupters of the religious rites.[13] In Polynesia, clowns appear at the Hura (family ball) when the young girls are tired of dancing and need a rest. The clowns provide comic relief, as Roman clowns did, by burlesquing the dance steps.[14]

Arab clowns use costuming that is hundreds of years old. They shave their entire heads, except for one long tuft of hair, and paint their faces in set patterns. Although no slapstick is used, blows are given with cupped hands.[15]

Secular Clowns in Europe and America

Today the direct religious significance of secular clowns and fools in Western culture is minimal. While they do speak to the core of being human, it is not deliberately religious. The circus as it is known today began in 1768 in Europe, and was largely an equestrian show.[16] What clowning there was was done on the backs of horses. But because it was only a one-ring show, the intimacy allowed the clowns to talk to their audiences located only a few feet away.

Joe Grimaldi made the image of the clown popular in England in the early 1800s. His greatness came from his inventiveness, especially in regard to comic acrobatics. Although he never worked in a circus, many of his theater and music hall skits are used there today, and all clowns are known as "joeys" in his honor.

A short while after Grimaldi, a clown known as "Footit" perfected the skill of speaking clown jokes. He worked with another clown known as "Chocolate," and they began the tradition of clowns working in pairs in Western society.   When the circus reached America, the mediums clowns had available to work in were reduced. Emmett Kelly reports that circuses in Europe were one-ringers, but quickly became three rings in America. Because of the large spaces involved, clowns no longer could talk and sing to the audience. They could only pantomime. Also, because the intimacy was lost, clowns became only another part of the fast-paced action.[17]

Clown performers began to change characters throughout the show, instead of working as one character. They also used only basic styles of clowning that involved large movements, large objects, and clothing that was either much too large or much too small. Since a person sitting in the back of the stands of the three-ring circus could no longer distinguish individual clowns or their facial expressions, solo clown acts were ineffective. Their movements were lost. Such individuals had included Poodles Hanneford, Felix Adler, Otto Griebling, and Emmett Kelly.[18] Kelly, in particular, overcame the problem of distance by working in the stands among the people.

Types of Modern Clowns

There are three major types of secular clowns. The first is the "white-face" who exaggerates the qualities of childlikeness. This clown presents an image of being vulnerable, caring, trusting, sometimes mischievous, and a bringer of joy. The whiteface is a descendant of Pierrot.[19]

The second type of clown is the "sad-face." This one draws out the caring instinct in people, and tries to have the audience respond by trying to cheer the clown up.[20]

The third type is the "Auguste" or "grotesque."

> The grotesque clown, in physical appearance and action, exaggerates the human condition. Best known for things which don't work, the prat-falls, the grotesque clown is often viewed by the fellow clowns as "the one who can stand." Despite the falls, there always seems to be resources, transcendent, personal, or even coming from the audience, which enable the clown to stand. This does not mean the clown will not fall again. When [the clown] does, however, the clown always has the potential to stand again. This is a magnificent illustration of grace.[21]

Charlie Chaplin and Buster Keaton were Auguste clowns. Emmett Kelly combined all of the basic clown types. He used the sadness and gentleness of Pierrot and the sad-face, and the clothing and prat-falls of the Auguste. He called his clown "Weary Willie." In general, Auguste clowns appear in pairs with whiteface clowns, in the manner of Footit and Chocolate. The whiteface plays the straight part, is rational and respectable, and plays by the rules. The Auguste plays the comic part, is simple-minded, and violates the rules. By having this basic dichotomy in the status of each clown, the pair can play just about any situation in society.[22] In this century, such pairs have included Weber and Fields, and Laurel and Hardy.

Emmett Kelly

One of the few clowns to have a recognizable character in the American circus was Emmett Kelly. He is also one of the few clowns to write a book about his life. This provides a rare, inside view into the world and art of clowning. He worked as a clown into the 1960s.

Clowns, Kelly says, try to catch people by surprise, and to have them laugh at the unexpected. A skit will begin as something serious, but end in a ridiculous way. For example, a person is sawed in half. But when the halves are separated, two midgets get up and run away.[23]

A good number of his skits left the audience feeling sad, yet empowered. He would stare soulfully at women while nibbling on a wilted cabbage leaf, and of course the women would laugh at him. He'd try to sweep up a spotlight with a broom, and have a terrible time. When cracking open a peanut with a sledge hammer, he'd look heart-broken when nothing is left but powder. And he would fall hopelessly in love with a female aerialist, worship her from the ground below, only to be rejected when she comes down to applause and the arms of the ringmaster.[24] Kelly describes his character as a sad character who is serious about everything, but that no matter how hopeless the situation looks, still hopes. He felt that his clown was so popular because many people often felt sad and beaten down, and that by laughing at him, and thus at their own situations, they found hope for trying again.[25] Although Kelly made no pretense about being a religious figure, he had a genuine concern about touching people inside. He saw that humor had transcendent and healing powers. He wanted to show people that no matter how bad things were, no matter he or anyone else made, there was still reason to hope.

With the coming of television and movies, clowns gained new mediums. Charlie Chaplin, Buster Keaton, Harold Lloyd (1903-1971), the Marx Brothers, and Red Skelton (b. 1913) were some of the clowns to become popular through them.

Buster Keaton and Charlie Chaplin

Buster Keaton (1895-1966) and Charlie Chaplin (1889-1977) made it big in the movies by using physical comedy. Bill Irwin and Geoff Hoyle, via the Pickle Family Circus, have continued the tradition.

Keaton's trademarks were his poker face, his flat hat, and his unbelievable acrobatic skills. No matter what happened to him, his body survived the blow, and his face never showed any emotion. He went over waterfalls and survived with only a bump on his head. In *Steamboat Bill, Jr*, houses were falling down all around Keaton while a tornado blows him down the street. In *The General*, he leaps from a moving train to the tracks to the firebox to the locomotive to the tracks so often and so effortlessly that the audience is left in a state of worn-out delight.

It seems as though Keaton's body is not united with his mind. His body is always a step behind, and his feet always trying to catch up. The audience feels it too: an inner tension that invites participation. Kevin Bradt says Keaton is "caught between thought and instinct which leaves him dumb-founded and bewildered in his classic dead-pan."[26] It is an inner struggle to decide what he wants to do first. He is not afraid to run away when he is afraid. He is also not afraid to take cheap shots at those who are out to do him harm. Either the improbable happens to save him from danger,or else he does the physically impossible. Either way, the audience responds openly to Keaton's tenacity and durability.

Charlie Chaplin struggled to move beyond what life gave him. Unlike Keaton, Chaplin struggled against "external forces of authority, conformity and power intent on oppressing and destroying the innocent of the world."[27] Chaplin knew who he was and what he wanted. There was no inner confusion. The problems came from society. His was "the terrible pathos of a beautiful soul trapped inside a hungry, battered body, barely surviving at the dead ends of society."[28] He may have been reduced to tears, but never to despair. Chaplin's clothes were shabby, but they were once elegant. He wrote this about his character:

> That ostume helps me to express my conception of the average [person], of almost any [person], of myself. The derby, too small, is a striving for dignity. The moustache is vanity. The tightly buttoned coat and the stick and his whole manner are a gesture toward gallantry and dash and "front." He is trying to meet the world bravely, to put up a bluff, and he knows that too. He knows it so well that he can laugh at himself and pity himself a little.[29]

He is the guy who puts out his hand to the bully, gets punched for it, yet comes back to do it all over again.

While Keaton risks killing himself with his stunt work and inner conflicts, "Charlie risks being killed by society for the prophetic, self-sacrificing, anarchic call to life only he hears and faithfully proclaims."[30] Both of them reach out to people who do not yet have their lives together.

The Marx Brothers were a tour de force of physical comedy and verbal wit. But instead of one person trying to survive a harsh world, there are three crazy people running around re-making the world in their image. In one of their movies, Groucho Marx invites people into his shipboard cabin until it is stuffed. Each person has an excellent reason for being in the room. Finally the dignified matron arrives, as she usually does sometime during each of their movies. When she opens the stateroom door, a flood of people come tumbling out, and we are reminded how improbable such an event really is. Yet, how often have we been trapped in cramped quarters until it seems the room would burst! Our laughter here helps heal the memory of that past discomfort and anger.

Marcel Marceau

Mime often conjures up images of people in black pants, suspenders, and whiteface making fun of people, but it is more than that. France is probably the home of classical mime, where Marcel Marceau and Etienne Decroux both have schools; but North America is the home of street mime. In recent years, Shields and Yarnell have done much to bring the image of mime to the North American public. Today in most major cities, it's not unusual to see mimes in various garb entertaining people on street corners. As with clowning, there are varieties of mime. The San Francisco Mime Troupe doesn't do much mime anymore. Their social and political satire is presented in a guerrilla theater format. Leonard Pitt has studied the abstract purity of classical mime with Decroux in Paris, and the earthy humor of masks with Kakul in Bali. A performer and teacher of mask and mime in Berkeley, Pitt sees the need to balance technique with humor.

Mime is a cousin of clowning. In the strict sense, the intent is the same, but the techniques differ. Clowning tends to tell with broad strokes, while mime focuses on the bare essentials. In reality, it is not unusual to see the exacting illusions of mime blend with the gross exaggerations of clowning. Generally what is said about clowning in this book holds true for miming. Probably the best known mime today is Marcel Marceau.

"Bip" is Marceau's main character, and is much like the characters Charlie and Keaton put in the movies. No matter what he tries Bip fails. Marceau says, "In each case it is the innocent Bip, misunderstood by the world, always dreaming, always trying to fit in, never quite succeeding."[31]

With the waning of the circus in America, fewer people were going into clowning. Realizing what their circus would be without clowns, Ringling-Barnum founded an eight-week "Clown College" in New York City in 1968.[32] There they train people to be apprentice clowns in the Ringling style. After graduation the new clowns work in the "specs" (spectacular numbers) until they are replaced by new apprentice clowns.

Circuses are making a comeback today. At last count, there were over 230 circuses in the U.S., ranging in size from the very small quarter-ring circus of Nick Weber's Royal Lichenstein Sidewalk Circus" to the mammoth Ringling Brothers and Barnum and Bailey Circus.

Russian Clowns

In Russia's recent history, clowns have been important commentators. In contrast, Ringling Brothers tell their clowns to stay away from all political and "vulgar" subject matter.[33] This connection in politics began in Russia in the 1880s as an extension of the medieval court jesters. When the czars were in power, only the clowns, or the political jesters in the guises of fools, could get away with political criticism.[34]

With the coming of the Russian Revolution in 1917, the Bolshevik forces at the front lines were entertained and inspired by Vitaly Lazarenko, a circus clown. He was called the "first shock-brigadier of clowning." In a political skit by another clown Vladimir, the falling value of the ruble was the focus of concern. His partner in this skit is a real pig.

> Vladimir asked Chushka to pick up a silver ruble from the floor. The spectators began to titter when the trained pig found it difficult to execute such a simple trick. Then Durov dryly commented, "Ladies and gentlemen, what can you expect from a pig if even the Minister of Finance can't raise the ruble?"[35]

In a non-political sketch by the Russian clown duet, Bim-Bom, called "The Laugh," they did nothing but laugh. But they laughed in such a comical fashion that it became contagious and the audience ended up joining in. "It was even reported that during the Russian civil war group of battle-fatigued soldiers made the near-fatal mistake of listening to a recording of this routine and were sent into a state of utter delirium as a result."[36]

The Stalinist era brought an end to such political satire and comic buffoonery in exchange for "social realism." In reality, this realism amounts to a little more than propaganda. Those who persist in playing political commentator simply disappear. A talented mime in the tradition of Marceau, Leonid Yengibarov of Armenia, has not been heard from since 1972, and is presumed to be dead.[37]

The history of clowns throughout the world is as varied as the needs of people. Whatever people take too seriously, clowns are around to make fun of it. And whatever is not taken solemnly enough, clowns try to correct the imbalance. There are political clowns, social clowns, religious clowns, and clowns who aim at simply entertaining people. Often they disappear for a while when societies decide that thinking is more important than feeling. Yet clowns always manage to show up again. They are a part of humanity. A modern clown, Otto Griebling, concludes:

> If you find yourself able to make people laugh, it is God's gift. You have to do everything from the bottom of your heart. I don't go in for slapstick. I let the emotion come from inside and penetrate the eyes. I'm the same man underneath, I'm always part of the human tragicomedy.[38]

CHAPTER 3
Old Testament Clowns

[Zorba came with a] savage bubbling laugh from a deep, deep
well-spring deeper than the bowels of humans], a laugh which at
critical moments spurted and
was able to demolish (did demolish) all the barriers — morality,
religion, homeland — which [those] wretched [poltroons],
[humans], had erected around [them] in order to hobble with full
security through [their] miserable [smidgens] of life.
— Nikos Kazantzakis, *Zorba the Greek*, p. 152

When a Christian looks at the history of the Jewish and Christian
religions, it is not immediately evident how many fools belong to both
groups. It's not that careful study is required. It is more a matter of
working through the pious layers of interpretations that have accumulated over the centuries like so much thick molasses. A non-
Christian often sees the puns, jokes, put-ons, and funny incongruities.

Humor is basically humor, and clowning is basically clowning,
whether it is done in the marketplace or in the church. It should come
as no surprise that the same transforming power that is at work in tribal
and secular clowning is also at work in clowning done in Christianity.
The same pattern of juxtaposing two seemingly different and separate
realities upon each other still works to reveal new visions.

Jewish Humor

Since Christianity has its roots in the Jewish faith, and since Jesus
was born and raised a Jew, it is helpful to have some notion of what
Jewish humor is about. The sense of humor is strong in the Jewish people. They are a people who know what it is to be a minority and what it
is to be persecuted. Humor is one way they, as most persecuted people, have traditionally dealt with abuse. Leo Rosten says, "In nothing is
Jewish psychology so vividly revealed as in Jewish jokes. The style and
stance of its humor reflect a culture, I think, no less than its patterns of
shame, guilt, hostility, and approval."[1] The background of many comedians in the U.S. as either Jewish or black indicates that humor is an effective way to deal with and partially overcome feelings of being
powerless. In 1951 Christopher Fry surmised this when he wrote that
comedy was not an escape from truth, but from despair — "a narrow
escape into faith."[2]

Elie Wiesel knows how important it is to laugh; to celebrate even when life's circumstances seem to prohibit such. In Russia he found that Jews are sometimes commanded to engage in celebration, lest despair overwhelm them.[3] Wiesel, himself, learned this lesson. He survived the Nazi concentration camps of Auschwitz and Buchenwald and today tells the stories about Jewish life in the shadow of the Holocaust.

One of his collection of stories is called *Souls on Fire*. The image is a surprising one, for it is an image that rekindles the overwhelming memories of the horror camps. Yet the Jewish religion, especially the Hasidic movement that began in the 18th century, "looks at our expectations, scoffs at them, and tosses them aside." Note the unexpectedness of this image, since fire (post-holocaust) has been the image of destruction. And yet the image of souls on fire, Robert McAfee Brown says, 'is a positive image — of souls ablaze with the glory of God.'[4] Wiesel uses something of hasidic humor to introduce "unexpected logic into a situation, thus making the situation transformable."[5] Something can now be done. There's hope where none existed before.

The use of humor by Jews in the time of Jesus may not differ greatly from how humor is used today, largely because the Jewish religion has taken great pains to preserve its traditions and culture. Rosten says Jewish humor is and has been largely cerebral. "It is, like Sholom Aleichem's, reason made mischievous, or, like Groucho Marx's, reason gone mad. Jewish jokes drape their laughter on logic — in despair."[6] Elie Wiesel offers an example of Hasidic humor that shows a relationship with God that is both respectful and Two-way:

> [Levi-Yitzhak of Berditchev] offered God a bargain: "We shall give you our sins and, in return, You will grant us Your pardon. By the way, You come out ahead. Without our sins, what would You do with Your pardon?"[7]

In the Jewish traditions and literature, fools and clowns have made their presence felt and respected. The Talmud tells this story about clowns:na

> . . . a Rabbi one day met Elijah, the wandering spirit of prophecy in Hebrew lore and asked who was worthy of eternal life. Elijah pointed to two clowns [who] were amusing the bystanders. The Rabbi, a serious fellow, showed great astonishment. "Scorn them not," said the Prophet, "it is always their habit, even when not performing for hire, to cheer the depressed and sorrowful. By their merry talk they cause sufferers to forget grief."[8]

Martin Buber offers an example about fools. People known as the "Fools of God" appeared in the ghettos of Eastern Europe, continuing a tradition found with the Chinese Buddhists, the Sufis, and the disciples of St. Francis of Assisi. They were, Buber writes, 'human beings who, because of their undamaged relationship with God, have quitted the rules and regulations of the social order, although they continue to participate in the life of their people."[9] These fools, like clowns in the circus, exist outside the rules that hold society together. But by listening to a greater reality, and by caring for their people, they hold society together with a stronger glue.

Fools appear in Jewish literature as the "schlemiels" and the "schlimazls." These are the people who continually find misfortune and injury at the hands of others. Saul Bellow's translation of the Yiddish tale, *Gimpel and Fool*, is an example of this.

In my own tradition, Christianity constantly flirts with making religion a ponderous bore. It too easily is willing to overlook the reality that, as Margie Brown says, the "Bible folk were a family of foolish stumblers."[10]

Old Testament Fools: Sarah and Abraham

One of the early examples of genuine humor in the Old Testament is the story of Sarah and Abraham, recorded in Genesis 17. God comes along one day and tells them they are going to have a baby. The Almighty does not even ask if they are interested. "Yes, yes," pious Christians today solemnly and rationally nod their heads: "This story definitely shows how God can work miracles, for Abraham and Sarah were terribly old. Sarah was 90 years old, or something like that, and Abraham was at least 100. Their ages safely put both of them beyond any childbearing capabilities by any sane-minded person. When they heard the news, the soon-to-be-parents fell on their knees and worshiped the Almighty God for the graciousness of this miracle." Really?

It is not hard to imagine Christians recounting the Biblical story in this way. Unfortunately, this is not how the story reads. For one thing, Sarah and Abraham laughed. God should have struck them both down for such inappropriate behavior. After all, Mary, the mother of Jesus, did not laugh when she was told she was going to have a baby. Or did she? Perhaps the Gospel writers wrote the laughter out. Whether they did or not, the Old Testament records that Abraham and Sarah both laughed.

Floyd Shaffer notes that this type of laughter exhibits an active trust relationship.[11] Do Christians today have enough faith to laugh at God, or with God? Or do Christians guard their reactions to the sometimes outrageous stunts that God pulls now and then? I wonder which kind of reaction is in line with Old Testament faith? Shaffer says this kind of relationship allowed Abraham and Sarah to share all their feelings and emotions with God: laughter and tears, joys and sorrows, and sarcasm and anger. Why? Because they knew they were loved.[12]

Sarah and Abraham not only laughed, they laughed so hard that they fell on their faces and not on their knees in awe. This is pure slapstick. If this was part of a circus routine, people would be rolling out of their seats and into the aisles. Why not laugh here? "God is such a tease," Sarah and Abraham must have thought, thinking that God was playing with them. Imagine their surprise when the fetus began kicking in her womb!

With the birth of the child, the parents had another opportunity to be solemn and proper. Naming children was a sacred matter for the Jewish people. A person's name was to be the summary of that person's spirit and essence. It's merest mention was enough to make that person fully present. The pious people of today would probably name the child "Miracle" or "Grace," or some Hebrew word that stands for "Blessed-gift-bestowed-upon-us, the-unworthy-parents." But God took no chances and named the child "Isaac." Sarah and Abraham must have had another laughing fit, for "Isaac" means "Laughter" in Hebrew. Perhaps God chose the name to remind the parents of the joke that had been played on them. Perhaps God wanted to remind them not to forget to laugh, even in the presence of a miracle. What clowns! Sarah, Abraham, and Laughter. And God.

What is working in this story, among other matters, is the juxtaposition of two seemingly conflicting realities. In the language of Emmett Kelly, it is making the unexpected happen. The first reality is that women bear babies. The second reality is that old women do not, especially when impregnated by old men. Also, it is assumed that solemnity is the only way to approach God. One does not joke around with the Omnipotent One. With Abraham and Sarah the two realities come together. They catch us by surprise. If we are sharp, we laugh. If we let some pious interpretations lead us, we solemnly pray. I don't think it is going to far to say that Abraham and Sarah were saved by Laughter.

There is also the matter of our laughing at the reactions of Sarah and Abraham to the unexpected news. We don't. And that's the problem. We should be able to laugh at God so hard that sometimes we fall on our faces. So often we maintain a stiff, and somewhat artificial, relationship with God, rather than a flexible, nurturing one that allows give and take. We favor the stiff because flexibility requires that we acknowledge our failings, and we don't like to do that.

The Prophets

Elsewhere in the Old Testament, the attitude of Sarah and Abraham is continued. In what was written about the prophets, those noble old bastions of holiness, there are portraits that are not easily understood by rational minds. The closer we look, the harder it is to believe that they were entrusted to be primary intermediaries between God and the people. What they were doing was simply continuing the role of the fool in culture. Fools may act strangely. They may not even be fools but choose the guise for one reason or another. There are, of course, people who simply do not understand how to live as responsible citizens in a society and do strange things simply because they do not know better.

Fools like the Hebrew prophets understand quite well what is going on. Sometimes they understand too well, and this lands them in trouble. They choose the garb of a fool either to hide their wisdom until the proper moment for revelation comes, or just to make a point visually. The prophets' adopted foolishness did not make them easy to get along with. As Frederick Buechner says, "There is no evidence to suggest that anyone ever asked a prophet home for supper more than once."[13]

Israel had a long relationship with God before the prophets arrived on the scene. They came at a time when the Israelites were going secular and learning to do without Yahwah. Like gang-busters the prophets came charging in demanding that the people obey the old traditions and uphold the original covenant. And yet, although prophecy came to the prophets, and the prophets drew material from old traditions, they still had to interpret it all with their lives. They had to enflesh it with skin and bone, and re-clothe it in the language and images of their people. So God's message was tempered by the temperament and character of each prophet. Abraham Heschel states, "The prophet is a person, not a microphone . . . [The prophet] speaks from the perspective of God as perceived from the perspective of [the prophet's] own situation.[14]

The prophets had to live with the idea that people might die if they held back on their messages. In the same way, clowns see people shriveling up for lack of laughter, for taking business too seriously, and for ptting too much value on order and calm. Prophets, like clowns, were "[individuals] who said "No" to [their] society, condemning its habits and assumptions, its complacency . . . Their words are onslaughts, scuttling illusions of false security, challenging evasions, calling forth faith to account, questioning prudence and impartiality."[15] Their ways were seldom gentle. Rather, they were dramatic, direct, and violent.

More in the vein of the Sioux Heyhokas, who also blended foolishness with religion, the prophets acted in ways that people in their day found hard to understand, let alone accept. The prophets ate bugs and hid in trees. Isaiah walked around naked and barefoot for three years as a warning against allying with Egypt (Isaiah 20:2-3). Jeremiah walked around naked with an ox-yoke on his shoulders. Amos, a shepherd from the Southern Kingdom, dared to go north into the rich and proud Northern Kingdom and preach social-action sermons about sharing with the poor and the hungry. Hosea married a whore. When she got tired of him, she went back to work. Hosea had to pay the going rate just to have time with his wife. Ezekiel is told by God to cook his food over human excrement (Ezekiel 4:12). He also saw skeletons moving in the desert, and wheels spinning in the air. These are not normal people, not sensible like you and me. Look at the oddities recorded in these accounts:

> One day some city boys followed along behind the prophet Elisha calling him "Bald-head!" Elisha summoned two she-bears, who tore forty-two of the city boys limb from limb. He then continued on his way to keep an appointment on Mount Carmel. (2 Kings 2:23-25)

The Prophet Jeremiah showed a clay pot to a crowd of Judeans and told them it represented Judah. Then he smashed it to smithereens and told them that this was an expurgated version of what God had in mind to do them. (Jeremiah 19) He was right.

In a dream the prophet Ezekiel ate a copy of the Bible, thumb-index and all, to show how sweet as honey was the word of God. (Ezekiel 3:1-3)[16]

Are these nice, sane people?

It is not recorded if any of the prophets either were mad or went mad. They were called mad for having a different view of reality. And once the people decided the prophets were mad, they did not have to be listened to anymore. One would suspect that some of them did go mad by the end of their ministries, driven so by the stress of the unusual job, and the constant abuse. Hosea said, "The prophet is a fool, the person of the spirit is mad, because of your great iniquity and great hatred." (Hosea 9:7)

The way some of them died is also reminiscent of how other fools in history have died who spoke the truth too directly or too often. Jeremiah was first thrown into a cesspool, which should have killed him, before he was kidnapped to Egypt where he probably died. Isaiah was sawed in half, according to rumor. John the Baptist lost his head over a dancing girl, and Ezekiel seems to have just disappeared.

These are the kinds of people Christians call their heroes. Are Christians to live as they did? Clowns and fools, every one of them.

Adam and Eve

What is a clown? Most authorities say the word "clown" comes from the Anglo-Saxon word "clod." Floyd Shaffer connects this meaning with Genesis:

> A clod was a lowly, down-to-earth person, like a lump from the soil. And no matter how you read the opening chapter of Genesis, it always comes out the same way: God loved a clod. God breathed divine spirit into it, made it an object of love, and said that it was good![17]

Look at Eve and Adam. What do they do? They are created. They name the animals and plants and everything else, and make a few bad choices, but nothing serious. Then they make a rather large mistake. They eat the apple. So soon in the beginning, after finishing only one job, they goof. What clods! And as most of the Protestant reformers gleefully pointed out every chance they got, humans have not risen above this level since. No matter how hard we try, we still come up being clods. Yet this is not an altogether bad situation. Shaffer continues,

> The nearest equivalent in the New Testament Greek is the word "doulous," which means "servant." Of all the words in the New Testament this one is the lowest form of the servant, the one with no apparent power. This is the word Christ used on the night before his crucifixion, and at other times when he held forth the "servant" as a life style for his followers.[18]

So a clown is a servant; and a servant in the manner of Jesus. Maybe there is something theological about clowns in the church.

What does the rest of the Old Testament say about clowns and fools of faith? Are all the important people clowns? No, but many of them have a strong sense of humor.

Gideon

In the book of Judges (chapter 7) the wise rationality of people is confronted and confounded in a story about Gideon.[19] If one of our church committees had been involved, it would have been all over for the Hebrews. As it was, Gideon was instructed by God to take a small group of people armed with clay pots, horns and flaming torches. Modern-day equivalents would be kazoos and flashlights.[20] It seems somewhat unwise to go into battle without having something to fight with. This is not at all the way to proceed when trying to save one's people from extinction. Yet, this was what God wanted to do, so Gideon went along.

In the dead of the night this unpretentious force surrounded the camp. They smashed their jars, blew their kazoos, and held up their flashlights. The enemy camp woke up in a panic, and the battle was over. Once again, apparent foolishness worked out far better than the accepted method. The unexpected won. Following the accepted rules of combat would have resulted in many Hebrews dying, and perhaps the battle for the nation's survival lost. Laughter, clods, and kazoos. What is God up to?

Other fools in the Old Testament include Jacob the trickster, who himself is tricked; Noah, who built an enormous boat miles from any decent-sized body of water; and Balaam the seer, who is taught some wisdom by his ass. Even God is sometimes seen as being less than wise. An example of this is when God is bargained down in regards to the number of people needed to save Sodom and Gomorrah: "Well, okay. If you can find just fifty . . . or ten righteous people . . . oh, I don't know how many. But find some, and I'll change my mind about destroying the cities. Again."

CHAPTER 4
New Testament Foolishness

> Like the jester, Christ defies customs and scorns crowned
> heads. Like a wandering troubador he has no place to lay his head.
> Like the clown in the circus parade, he satirizes existing authority
> with regal pageantry when he has no earthly power. Like a minstrel
> he is costumed by his enemies in a mocking caricature of royal
> paraphenalia. He is crucified amidst sniggers and taunts with a sign
> over his head that lampoons his laughable claim.
> — Harvey Cox, *Feast of Fools*, p. 140

Jesus' ministry and life were filled with foolishness and laughter.
John the Baptist played his straight man."[1] Jesus poked fun at the
overly-religious, confounded the expectations of the common people,
and often shocked his disciples with his preposterous images and
lifestyle. He was the master of imagination. He kept saying, "What if
this was *that* way?" and the new possibility just rolled out. Unfortunately
a lot of them also rolled past people because they were not looking in
the right direction. They were still trying to fit Jesus' holistic teachings
into their nicely organized boxes. Not only are the parables of Jesus
prime examples of his humor, but so are his other teachings.

Elton Trueblood challenges the conventional picture of a Christ
who never laughed. The Gospel needs to be freed "from the excessive
sobriety," he says, "which is provided by the authors and by us . . .
Christ was not always engaged in pious talk."[2] Frederick Buechner
heard a sermon 20 years ago that broke the pious image and made
faith possible for him. The preacher was saying that 'Christ is crowned
among confession, tears, and great laughter.' When the preacher said
the words "great laughter," Buechner reports, suddenly 'the Great Wall
of China crumbled and Atlantis rose up out of the sea,' and he
believed.[3]

The humor that most often comes through in the gospels is of
irony and sarcasm. Paradoxes and the preposterous also are common.
Yet the rich sense of a broader humor — of jest, playfulness, and puns
have been eliminated from the accounts for fear of making Jesus appear less than serious.

It is difficult to assess the humor that has been eliminated from the gospel accounts. It is known that the gospel writers reworked the original material in order to address the specific concerns of their different audiences, much as the prophets had done before them. Some humor was probably lost here. One would also expect that a person who loved to play with the language as much as Jesus did, would have told a great many puns in his native Aramaic. Puns are always hard to preserve in translation into English.

Some humor is also timely. Allusions to certain images that used to make roll in the aisles, make no sense at all to people of another time and another culture. People centuries later look on these confusing allusions as facts. Instead of laughing, they memorize. Fortunately some of this rumor can be recaptured by studying the times and dynamics of when the phrase was used. An example of this is the comparison of the Kingdom of Heaven to a mustard shrub. Funny, isn't it? This example will be explained later on. Chances are today, that if a passage is either dull or does not make sense, something humorous is going on.

Confounding Expectations

Jesus likes to play with juxtapositions. He makes worlds crash together, and slaps paradox on top of paradox. For example, he comes along and sets all the expectations people have for the Messiah on their heads. Yes, Jesus was the savior who was expected; but he was not the *type* of savior people were looking for. Some were waiting for a great military leader to rise up and drive out the Roman Imperialist Army. They got someone who would rather die than fight with arms; someone who was more concerned with interpersonal relationships than about governmental politics. Some expected a great religious leader to do the work and usher in the new world of God. What they received was someone telling them to usher it in themselves. Even the small group of women and men who tramped around with him were not sure who he was, or what he wanted.

First of all, the savior of the world is born into a low-rider situation. This is funny because it is incongruous. But who laughs at the incongruity of it? Who even smirks a little? It is two worlds clashing and saying that the result makes sense. Couldn't the Son of God do better? People in Jesus' day realized how preposterous such an event was. They had a phrase for it. "Can anything good come out of Nazareth?" Then they laughed. Very natural, like telling Polish jokes have been, rightly or wrongly, for so long.

Second of all, Jesus rides into Jerusalem, in what is his coronation parade, not on a proud horse, but on a donkey, a beast of burden, not of kings; and on a small donkey at that. A modern equivalent is for a world leader to ride in the inaugural parade not in the traditional black cadillac, but on a motorcycle, and on a moped at that. A modern playwright has come up with another startling image for this occasion:

> Christ on a bicycle. You can see that. You can't see him driv-
> ing a Jaguar. Or an Avenger. Or a Sting-ray. A car is just a hard
> shell of aggression, for the soft urban mollusc to secrete itself in. It's
> a form of disguise. All its parts are hidden. No wonder they are us-
> ing them as bombs. It's a logical development. A bicycle hides
> nothing and threatens nothing. It is what it does, its form is its func-
> tion. An automobile is a weapon of war.[4]

Thirdly, the genealogy of Jesus is not at all the pure, pristine roll
call of honor it is frequently assumed to be. Doug Adams points out
that a great deal of humor is missed when we forget who the people
are. Mixed right in with the noble, righteous people who gave Jesus
good genes, are prostitutes, murderers, thieves and adulterers.[5]

Other examples of paradox include the Sermon on the Mount,
where the first shall be last and the last shall be first philosophy is
spelled out (Matthew 5);the taking on of a yoke on a symbol of
freedom (Matt 11:29); and the blind leading the blind (Luke 6:39)
Jesus' beatitudes are really anti-beatitudes, for they play against the notion of what beatitudes were supposed to be — blessings. The meek in-
herit the earth? Really? In this world? And if they did, how long would
they be able to hold on to the earth before the greedy grabbed it back?
Paradoxes like these are needed to bring people to the "Ah hah" experiences of truly knowing something, and this can't be arrived at
logically.[6]

The preposterous was held up as a guide for faith. "It is easier for
a camel to go through the eye of a needle than for a rich man to enter
the Kingdom of God." (Mark 10:25). "Do not give dogs what is holy;
and do not throw your pearls before swine . . ." (Matt 7:6), which most
people have no plans to do anyway. It is even more preposterous to say
it to Jews because of their rejection of pork. What Jew raised pigs?[7]
And Jesus had a disciple take a coin out of the mouth of a fish. Makes
perfect sense, right?

A good example of Jesus' use of the preposterous is the story of
the Unjust Steward (Luke 16). Jesus is saying, in effect, that if the disciples want to get ahead they should cheat in a big way. "Don't steal *from*
the bank, He suggests," as Trueblood tells it, "steal the bank, and then,
instead of being punished, you will be respected." It will even be your
ticket into heaven. Those people who fail to see the humor here are
bound to make themselves look ridiculous.[8]

People's boxes are also smashed in the allusion of the Kingdom
of Heaven being like a mustard shrub. Jesus' listeners expected to hear
Heaven compared to the cedars of Lebanon, which are tall, strong, and
impressive to the eye. Instead, Jesus says, 'Heaven is like . . . the . . .
the mustard seed, which, although it is the smallest of seeds, grows up

to be the greatest of all . . . shrubs.' Shrubs! What happened to impressive trees? Jesus continues. 'And the shrub is so big that birds can nest in its shade.' Luke tries to restore the expected image by changing the original account that Mark told. Luke takes out the part about the mustard seed being the smallest of all seeds, changes "shrub" to "tree," and says that birds can nest in its branches, instead of on tne ground.[9]

Irony

Another aspect of Jesus' humor was the use of irony. Irony here means 'holding up to public view either vice or folly, but without bitterness or the attempt to harm.'[10] The encounter of Jesus with those who wanted to stone the woman caught in adultery is an example of this. Jesus simply asked the person who was without sin to throw the first stone. Then he doodled on the ground. Slowly the men slipped away.

In Matthew 22, the irony is a little sharper. The Pharisees have sent some of their followers to trip Jesus up, and turn the warmth of the people against him. They chose the highly volatile subject of paying taxes to the occupying forces of Rome.

They asked, "Is it right for Jews to pay taxes to the Roman Emperor?" Jesus has them show him one of the coins used to pay the tax. Usually modern sermons focus on Jesus' quick wit, his "pay to Caesar what is due Caesar, and to God what is due God," for the coin that is brought forth has Caesar's image on it. It obviously belongs to Caesar. Yet the deeper, ironic humor has been missed.

The Pharisees were always trying to avoid contamination with impure objects. Even to posses a coin, as they did, with the graven image of Caesar on it was a deep humiliation. Jesus really needed to go no further after the coin was produced. The damage was done. Those who came to humiliate were humiliated.[11]

Even though the records do not show it, I think that those with Jesus, as well as those people gathered around, guffawed as the Pharisees hurried away with their tails between their legs. Why has the humor of the passage not been recorded as being more obvious? Perhaps because the people the gospels were written to immediately understood the hilarity involved, and needed no instructions.

The Parables

For those who wanted to be told what to do, Jesus saved his parables. Christians today like to allegorize the parables. They like to figure out what Jesus really meant, and what the moral of the story is. Jesus almost seems bent on confusing and confounding people who looked to others for answers. Simply put, Jesus said, 'The Kingdom of God is within you. Follow the two great commandments of loving God, and loving your neighbor as yourself, and you'll do fine.' The gospel of

Mark flatly announces that the purpose of the parables is to confuse people (Mark 4:10-12).

Seldom was there a bottom line to the parables, seldom a decent ending. They were often left open-ended, with people waiting for the punch line that never came. There is a real danger of putting endings on parables that do not have any. John Dominic Crossan puts it succinctly: "Parable is paradox formed into story."[12] Adams adds that 'If we miss Jesus' humor, then we often not only miss the message, we may also receive the wrong message.'[13] Parables were never intended to be instruction manuals in miniature. They were intended to confuse the rational. Those who intend to understand God rationally are doomed to failure, for God is not rational.[14]

The following is a parable that was written in 1981. It has no centuries of religious interpretations piled on it. There is nothing that needs any explanation for people living today. It means what it says. Nothing more or less. Notice how the logic progresses, for it is indicative of how the logic progresses in Jesus' parables:

> A parable is like a prospective student asking the president of a seminary, "Why don't you have any women on the faculty?"
> The seminary president replied, "Adam was created first. First place teams win trophies. Trophies are displayed in cases. Cases are decided in court. Some tennis courts are made of clay. Clay is used in making ceramic dishes. Women wash dishes. If women wash dishes, they don't have time to teach. Therefore, we have no women on the faculty."[15]

The parables of Jesus were often responses to the questions themselves, not answers that provided ethical rules. They were given "to reveal the faultiness of our questions, of our ways of thinking, and the need for us to change.[16]

Jesus frequently talked in parables. He wanted to get away from people making idols out of his words and missing the underlying meanings that the words bore witness to. When Jesus told a parable, his listeners needed to check their logic at the door. Sometimes he did explain what his stories meant, although most of the explanations seem to be later additions by the gospel writers and others.   Crossan says "Jesus' was to announce the Kingdom's advent as demanding decision and response, life and action, but never articulating such action in detail within the parables themselves."[17] He says these parables do not set well with us because "We are frightened by the lonely silences."[18] We have to learn to react from feeling, rather than from thought. It is only through living the parables that we can come to understand them.

The challenge of Jesus and Paul was that obedience to moral precepts and laws does not lead to God, but rather God leads us to obedience. We have to search ourselves for the presence of God already moving within us.

Many of the parables were watered down, de-radicalized, and moralized over time by people who, ironically, sought to preserve them. These people changed the accounts, for example, by adding on explanations to difficult passages so that later generations would be able to profit from the insights of earlier ones. This is a nice goal, but one wishes they would have preserved their insights in another way. Trueblood says that the farther the church got away from the original, pre-gospel account of Jesus and his stories, the less humor there was.[19] It is doubtful if the church ever added any humor. Rudolph Bultmann and other New Testament scholars are convinced that the later teachings and preachings of the church were added in. Gunther Bornkamm points this out in the differences between Matthew's and Luke's accounts of the parable of the Great Supper (Matt 22:1ff, Luke 14:16ff). Matthew has clearly embellished the story.

Doug Adams points out that the humor in the parables is what people miss. For example, the Good Samaritan parable is actually a good news-bad news situation. The good news is that help is on the way. The bad news is that the help is coming from someone you detest. The parable is also more rightly called the parable of "the one in the ditch," for a Jew was asking the question, "What must I do to get into heaven?" Notice that there were only two roles the Jew could see himself playing. He could either be the person in the ditch, or be one of the people who passed by without stopping to help. Jesus tells him that if wants to get into heaven, he has to be the Samaritan in the story. He has to be someone he detests![20] Paradox; and challenge.

Peter was one who didn't understand Jesus' sense of humor in religious contexts. Adams says Peter had an Archie Bunker mind. He saw the world as being organized into neat, logical boxes. "Even the Gentiles must be circumcised!" Peter concluded. Jesus liked to poke fun at Peter because of his lack of imagination. In the Syro-Phoenician woman story, the woman asks Jesus to heal her daughter. Jesus said, "No." But as he does so he gives Peter a nudge in the ribs, as if to say, "I am only for the Chosen People, isn't that right Peter?" The woman persists, and Jesus becomes more blatant in his jesting, jabbing Peter harder in the ribs each time. The woman catches on and plays along. Her daughter is eventually healed. But Peter has to stand there and take it.[21] In many ways, Peter is a kind of court jester. He is the fool who asks the questions everyone else is dying to ask, but who don't dare.[22]

What have been taken as moral directions also contain surprises. When Jesus said, "turn the other cheek," he was not telling people to be submissive. In order to be submissive the person slapped would have to fall to the floor. Turning the other cheek is actually an act of defiance. It requires the head to be lifted up again, and the second cheek presented as a dare. "Carrying the bags a second mile" has the sense of 'If your boss tells you to work an extra hour for nothing, go one step further and go home for supper with your boss.' The last thing the boss wants is for you to come home for supper. The boss just wants work out of you, not a relationship. And "If someone asks you for your shirt, give the person your cloak also" is a quite a statement, for "cloak" means "underwear" in the original language, leaving the person naked.[23] All these statements Jesus said in response to questions that were wrongly asked, and had to do with "What must I *do* to enter heaven?"

When people in Jesus' day did not understand a parable he told, Jesus would explain by giving them a second parable. Now the confused people had two parables, none of which they understood. Jesus even did this with his disciples when they did not understand. "I tell you these things that you may understand — not like those dumb people out there!"[24] And they thought they had a privileged position!

The parables show how the people in the stories did or did not see beyond what the facts of the situation were. Did they see what was deeper, what was beyond the here and now? Did they preserve their neat, little boxes and hold to rules that preserved form but injured people, as the Pharisees did? Or did they break through rules in order to better care for the needs of people?

Jesus as Clown

Comparisons of Christ to a clown have been made throughout the 20th century. In his 1927 play, *Him*, e.e. cummings spoke of the clown as the Christ figure, "the one whom, more than we, knows the full breadth and depth of human life." Georges Rouault (1871-1958), a French expressionist painter, blended the influences of the circus and the French Catholicism to see Christ as a clown. Picasso painted languid harlequins. Fellini made films with magicians, acrobats, and clowns. Genet did a minstrel play, *The Blacks*. Becket wrote his *Waiting for Godot*. The Joffrey Ballet has presented Gerald Arpino's "The Clowns." And in literature, there is the clownish Oscar Mazerath in Gunter Grass's *The Tin Drum*.[25]

The image of Jesus as a clown made its way into recent imagination in the late 1960s and early 1970s. The movie, "The Parable," by Rolf Forsberg, was shown at the New York World's Fair in 1966. It presented Jesus as a clown sacrificing itself for others. Harvey Cox included a chapter on "Christ the Harlequin" in his 1969 book, *The Feast of Fools*. Then, in 1971, the rock musical "Godspell" came out, and for the first time a good many Christians encountered the old, yet new image. And many of them were shocked. In the late 1970s Monty Python came out with their movie, *The Life of Brian*, and people were shocked again. The movie really had little to do with Jesus, but many Christians were up in arms because the things *around* Jesus' time and life were parodied. Their reaction is a good indication of how much about Jesus was idolized. After all, the direct Christian significance of worshiping a shoe is very little.

When people are shocked, there is space for something new to happen. "Jesus a . . . a clown?" It seems a thing of contempt to make such a comparison; something to spit out behind the bushes and cover over with dead leaves. Yet modernizing the Image of Christ is nothing new.

Since the time of Christ the image of Christ has been changing. This is not to suggest that Christ is changing all the time. Christ remains the same. What is changing are the questions people ask of Christ. As Christ responds to these questions, new aspects of Christ are seen, and hence, new images. It is all part of the effort to believe that Jesus truly understands and speaks to what people are going through.

Theodore Ziolkowski has traced the shift in images of Jesus in literature written during the last 100 years. He says Christ has moved from being flesh and blood, to being a figure of myth and parody, to being a "bland construct twice-removed from its Gospel source."[26] The struggle to see Jesus as being both human and divine at the same time is a major source of the image search.

Tim Kehl has written perceptively on the theology of clowning.[27] He lists some of the images that have been important to various groups over the years:

> To the early Christians suffering persecution, Jesus was depicted as a *good shepherd* who would lead them to their heavenly reward. To medieval Christians bearing the gruesome ravishes of the black plague, Jesus was depicted as a *tortured figure on a cross* who shared their agony. To renaissance Christians who sought enlightenment, Jesus was depicted as a *great teacher or rabbi*.[28]

The image used to get a grasp on Jesus is important. If Jesus is presented as a shepherd to people who have never seen sheep, they have no reason to believe that God, or the church, has anything to say to them. Kehl believes there are two images that make sense for our world:

> The first is of Jesus the *revolutionary*, emerging out of the struggles for liberation taking place in the third world and among minorities here. The second is of Christ the *Clown*, emerging out of . . . [people's] search for authenticity in our modern mass society.[29]

People in the third world, and minorities in the first, are struggling to be heard and taken more seriously. People in the first world need to take themselves less seriously, and to listen to others. This is where the clown comes in.

Parallel Symbols and Roles for Clowns and Christ

Kehl points out several parallels between the message of the clown and the message of Christ. First of all, the clown is a *symbol of joy*: celebrating life, rejoicing in simple things, and delighting in children.[30] Jesus did the same. He ate and drank with the low life so much that he was called a drunkard and a glutton. It is clear Jesus drank alcoholic beverages and enjoyed eating food. He took time to notice flowers, and saw that their glory was greater than all of King Solomon's glory. And he told his disciples not send the children away, "for to such belong the kingdom of heaven." Joachim Jeremias maintains that the teaching of Jesus to be like children is *the* characteristic of God's future world.[31]

This is a celebrative perspective on life that some, like Nikos Kazantzakis' Zorba the Greek seem never to lose.

> I felt, as I listened to Zorba, that the world was recovering its pristine freshness. All the dulled daily things regained the brightness they had in the beginning, when we came out of the hands of the God. Water, women, the stars, bread, returned to their mysterious primitive origin, and the divine whirlwind burst once more upon the air . . . Everything seems miraculous to him, and each morning when he opens his eyes, he sees trees, sea, stones and birds, and is amazed.[32]

Second, the clown is a *symbol of hope*:

> One of the endearing features of clown humor is that the clown refuses to accept the limits of the possible. A clown will insist upon riding a bicycle whose wheels are out of kilter or to try to walk a slack tightrope. The audience knows that the poor clod will fall on his or her face. Sure enough he does, but he picks himself up, dusts himself off, and tries again. Sooner or later, through a combination of wit, ingenuity, and perseverance, the beleagured clown will succeed — to the great delight of the audience.[33]

This does not mean, however, that Charlie Brown will ever kick the football. It means that he still has hope he will.

Kehl points out the Christian equivalent. There are obstacles, frustrations and defeats in the life of every Christian. But there is also the eventual victory. The hope of Christians lies in the resurrection, when God refused to let Christ stay dead.[34] Christ not staying dead was a very clownish thing to do.

Third, the clown is a *non-conformist*, always challenging the conventional ways of thinking and acting. Clowns humble the exalted and exalt the humble.[35] Sioux Heyhokas, Hebrew prophets, Shakespearean fools, and Charlie Chaplin have all poked fun at the rules and traditions of societies, and have questioned their relevance. Likewise,

Jesus refused to be shackled by the traditions and conventions of His day. In an age of military might he counseled turning the other cheek. In an age of materialism, he urged his followers not to be anxious about possessions. In an age which exhibited women, he treated women as equals. In an age which looked down upon the poor and the outcast, Jesus cast his lot among them and dared to claim that there would be the salt of the earth and the light of the world. Like clowns before and after Him, He was banished from His hometown and crucified.[36]

Fourth, the clown is a *vulnerable lover* who expects only goodness from other people, and is hurt each time someone is rude, harsh, or too busy to care. Charlie Chaplin's character is like this.[37] In the same way, Jesus came with the message of love. He gave everyone the chance to be abusive and reject him.

Lastly, the clown is a *servant figure*, looking primarily to the needs of others before the needs of herself or himself. The clown seeks to bring joy to the depressed, and to make people more sensitive to each other.[38] In the same way, although he was not a clown in the sense of being an entertainer, Christ ministered to the needs of others.

Christ the clown is an important image today because Christians have lost their sense of joy and hope in the midst of seemingly endless inflationary and recessionary pressures. Christians have lost their zest for nonconformity and servanthood in a world that threatens to be blown up if one more nonconformist tries to run the show.

Paul and Fools for Christ

Paul is usually regarded as an unfunny fellow. He seems to be totally serious about spreading the message of Christ. If he were preaching on a street corner in any major city in the United States, just a quick glance at him would be enough to result in conversion. Yet, he too, had a sense of humor.

Much of his humor revolves around getting Christians to stop being so concerned with themselves, and asking questions like, "Who is the best Christian?" "How do I look? Am I fashionably religious without being pushy?" Paul uses his humor to move his readers away from their preoccupation with themselves to genuine concern for the welfare of others.

In the twelfth chapter of I Corinthians, Paul tries to make the people see that each of them is only a part of the body of Christ, and that they all need each other. Paul has body parts walking around the room, talking to each other. The humor should be obvious. If a giant ear is walking around without the benefit of an eye, it is going to be running into the walls, and falling down the basement steps. The giant nose is going to look like a snowplow on the floor. This is slapstick.

In the first chapter of I Corinthians, the issue is over who was baptized by Paul. Apparently some Corinthians were holding themselves up as being better Christians because Paul baptized them. Imagine a phone conversation between Paul and the Corinthians, and being able to hear only Paul's responses. Paul is speaking: "Baptized you? I did not! I never baptized anyone in Corinth. Wait a minute, I think I do remember baptizing Crispus and Gaius, but I'm not sure. It was so long ago. I do know that I didn't baptize anyone else. The household of Stephanas? Well, maybe I did, but I sure don't remember." The point Paul is getting to through his jesting is that it was only important that they be baptized. It does not matter who did the baptizing.[39]

Even though Paul's humor is not as obvious as the humor of Jesus, it is still there for the observing. Paul is also responsible for one of the most important phrases in the Bible for clowning: "We are fools for Christ's sake, while you are such sensible Christians." (I Cor 4:10). Paul clearly realizes that Christianity looks stupid when compared to the values of the world. What other religion counsels people to love their enemies, pray for those who persecute them, and take up an image of barbarous death as a symbol of hope? Yet Paul believed this folly with his life.

Christians usually resolve to work harder to be more like a fool like Paul when their pastors tell them to be "fools like Christ." Their notions of what this folly is take several paths, however. Etymologically, "fools" and "fun" are related to the same root word.[40] If Paul's statement is rephrased, interchanging the related words, we get something like this: "Christianity is a funny religion," and "We are to be clowns for Christ's sake." Say it this way and people's ears perk up. They begin to understand the original intent, and the core of what Paul was saying.

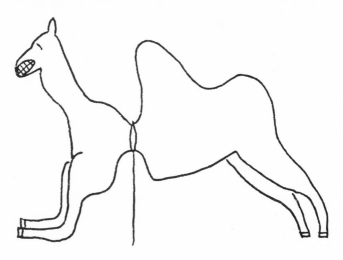

CHAPTER 5

Is There Fun After Paul?

> [Clowns] dare to live out [their] dreams, whatever the per-
> sonal cost. And such men (and women) are dangerous. They in-
> troduce a wild, unpredictable element into an otherwise tidy,
> soulless, prudential existence. This clown, Jesus, set up his
> kingdom in a tiny backwater of a great empire and declared a
> handful of peasants to be the pathfinders of a new humanity. He
> talked and practiced absurdities about loving one's enemies,
> cherishing the unlovable and unlovely, and claimed that giving and
> being forgiven are the most sublime human achievements. He es-
> tablished a fool's paradise, a colony of clowns — men and women
> who dared to live out their dreams, and pay whatever price was
> asked for them for the privilege.
> — Colin Morris, *Hammer of the Lord*, pp. 93-4

In the catacombs in Rome during the first century, when Christians were being tortured and burned in the streets above, humor was
very much alive. It needed to be. When the unfriendly neighbors up-
stairs began comparing Christ to a not so very bright donkey, the
catacomb Christians used the derogatory image to their benefit. They
painted it on the walls. The image was a donkey's head on Christ's
body as it hung on the cross, and they used it to remind themselves that
their faith would always look silly to the world. They knew that when it
no longer looked silly, their faith then would have been diluted with
worldly values.

Around 300 A.D., the church was drawing together the unity of
the faith at the expense of its original diversity. As it was preparing to set
the Trinitarian formula in cement, it condemned buffoons for singing
songs that were "impure," and for being "diabolic and frivolous."[1]
Shortly thereafter the church headed off on a path that would lead to
the stocking up of golden communion vessels and richly-jeweled vest-
ments. It can realistically be asked which path was the more diabolical.

Undoubtedly what the Roman theater had generated into was
largely responsible for the condemnation, for as it became more
elaborate, it also became more obscene. Emperor Helioglabus even
commissioned the realistic portrayal of sexual acts on stage. Hence St.
Augustine had good reason to comment: "The [person] who brings actors, mimes, and dancers, into [his or her] home does not know what a
gathering of demons enters along with them."[2] Yet, around the same
time, St. Athanasius said that "The risen Christ turns one's life into a

continual festival." Not only should we recognize the daily crosses involved in following Jesus, but we should also remember the promise of our resurrection in Christ — the joy.

In the sixth century, the Barbarians closed all the theaters and circuses, the mimes had to go to the streets to earn a living. The church continued to disapprove, and said that at the end of their lives, mimes were certain to burn in hell.[3]

Orthodox Fools

Aristotle laid important groundwork for the position of the fool in society. In his *Nicomachean Ethics*, he says there are three types of people. There is the boor, who takes life too seriously. There is the frivolous one who takes life lightly. And there is the grave-merry master who seeks balance. Their first two Aristotle considered buffoons. The third one he called the fool. Desiderius Erasmus celebrated Aristotle's grave-merry master in his *In Praise of Folly*. He also played the part to his renaissance society by exposing its hypocrisy and by celebrating the imperfections of human nature.[4]

Although not well known in the Western Christian Church, the term "fool" is regarded as a sacred vocation in the Eastern Orthodox churches. There it is a hagiographical category like "martyr," "virgin," and "confessor." "The *salos* or *yurosivy* (the Greek and Russian technical terms for 'holy fool') is regarded as one called by God to obey the words of the apostle: 'if any one among you thinks that they are wise in this age, let them become a fool that they may become wise.' (I Cor 3:18)."[5] It has its own liturgical material, as well.

The orthodox fool movement has its roots in the fourth century A.D., when people began going into the desert to live. These desert Mothers and Fathers saw in the inauguration of Christianity as a state religion by Constantine, a serious change in the dynamics of Christian life. No longer would Christians be pressured to hold to the bare-bone essence of faith because of persecutions. They saw the faith being watered down with compromises, much as the catacomb Christians had feared. So they headed for the desert where the physical life would once again be hard, and sensuality could be battled. There they had to trust in God for everything if they were to survive.

They intended to appear simple and foolish in the face of the growing worldly wisdom of secular Christians. There are many stories about people coming to a holy desert person, asking for spiritual guidance, and being rebuffed and repulsed by what they found. In one instance, a seeker came to Abbot Theodore of Pherme for words of wisdom. Theodore refused to say anything for three days, until the seeker finally went away disappointed. When questioned about this, the Abbot said the seeker was a "trader in words, and seeks to glory in the words of another."[6]

Unlike the desert people, the Orthodox fools had no caves and no garb. They wandered about serving people, and using every opportunity to publicly make fools of themselves. Yet whenever anyone needed help, the fools would volunteer. Such fools included St. Simeon Salos (d. 590?), who was known to have tied a dead dog to his belt and dragged it through the streets. One Sunday he went to Mass and extinguished the candles by throwing nuts at them. The angry reactions of the other worshippers helped Salos overcome the sin of pride. Through the guise of foolishness, Salos converted heretics with his humility, and healed the possessed.[7]

In the 1500s, the fool St. Philip Neri was forever playing tricks on people, and telling jokes. His sense of humor grew greater, rather than less, as his holiness grew greater. To him belonged the Gospel of Good Humor.[8]

There are three elements common to holy fools. The most important of them is their sense of Christocentricity. They are totally devoted to Jesus Christ and his teachings. They have chosen to live as he did, or at least that part of his life that was the subject of ridicule, debasement, and scorn. The second element is the eschatological nature of their ministry — always holding up the conflict between the values of this world and the values of the world Christ pointed to. Finally, the fools are all political, for any statement they make about society invariably has political ramifications. If there is one task holy fools take on with the mantle of itinerancy, it is the task of challenging their fellow Christians to remain faithful to the difficult folly of the cross.[9]

The golden age of all fools took hold in the thirteenth century. It may seem paradoxical that this age should coincide with the rise of St. Thomas and Scholasticism (which put a heavy premium on thinking). Yet St. Thomas made a distinction between the earthly wisdom that is substituted for God, and the "good folly that stands against this evil wisdom,"[10] much as St. Paul had done centuries before. Near the end of his life, Thomas took his ideas a step further into his own life, or rather, he was moved to do so. During Mass one day he felt the unexplainable urge to give up his weighty writing of exploring God and the movements of God. He would later confide that all of his writing amounted to 'so much straw before the wind.' He felt that even his massive *Summa Theologica* amounted to nothing. Karl Barth would come to feel the same way about his 12-volume *Church dogmatics*, which h would never finish, and which he realized he would never finish in his latter years.[11]

The thirteenth century was also the time of St. Francis of Assisi, who re-claimed the folly of the beggar's poverty and antics. He preached to the birds and animals; he kissed lepers and dared to catch leprosy himself; and he even tried to reform the elaborate structure inherent to the Roman Catholic church by doing without structure. His early Franciscans called themselves 'fools of Christ.' Francis had a deep suspicion of book knowledge, because he felt such knowledge only allowed people to respond from ideas in their heads, and not from the human experiences rooted in their hearts. Although he left orders before his death that no one be permitted to study higher education, one of his brothers disobeyed, and moved the Order in an educated direction. And although the original simplicity and foolishness of St. Francis was covered over, it does pop up here and there throughout the years since Francis lived.

Altogether thirty-six Russian Orthodox and six Greek Orthodox fools have been canonized. This is not to be used as a judgment for the Greeks because they had fewer fools, or for the Russians because they had more. The difference in numbers is due to the Russians connecting to the tradition earlier.[12]

The sixteenth century was the heyday for Russian fools. Among other events, one naked fool confronted Ivan the Terrible outside the gates of Pskov as Ivan was coming to tear the place down and do general destruction. The sight of the naked holy fool standing in the snow was enough to make Ivan decide to go elsewhere. The fool is also prominent in Russian literature. Among the numerous entries is 'Nicky, Nicky, Iron Nightcap' in Pushkin's *Boris Godunov*, the fools in Tolstoy's *Childhood, Boyhood, and Youth*, and the fools filling the pages of the writings of Dostoevski.[13]

The Medieval Feast of Fools

In France, the well-known Feast of Fools began in the twelfth century, as a New Year's religious celebration. For the Feast, the minor clergy dressed up in a variety of irreligious costumes, and made fun of the higher clergy, the various liturgical forms, and the rich, pompous people of the congregation. Criticism of the event was present from the beginning, especially whenever violence broke out. Matters came to a head in 1445, when the powerful Faculty of Theology at the University of Paris wrote a complaint. It signaled the beginning of the end:

> Priests and clerks may be seen wearing masks and monstrous visages at the hours of the office. They dance in the choir as women, panders or minstrels. They sing wanton songs. They eat black pudding at the horn of the altar while the celebrant is saying mass. They play dice there. They cense with stinking smoke from the soles of old shoes. They run and leap through the church without a blemish at their own shame. Finally they drive about the town and its theaters in shabby traps and carts; and rouse performances, with indecent gestures and versus scurrilous and unchaste.[14]

Another form of the Feast was the Feast of the Ass.[15] This played off of Mary and Joseph's flight into Egypt. A donkey would lead the procession through the city's streets. Then everyone, including the ass, went inside the church and the Mass was said. But instead of the congregation chanting its usual Latin phrases for the congregational response, they brayed back, "Hee-haw, hee-haw, hee-haw." Needless to say, such goings on were not likely to continue forever.

A third form was the Dance of Death. For this, one person dressed up as a skeleton, and led a procession of people around, as a way of reminding everyone that their time on earth was limited.

The impetus for the feasts seems to have come from the people. They wanted to feel more a part of the worship service, and wanted to break the dull solemnity of church matters with some fun. There was probably also some anger involved, as poor worshippers were tired of being pushed to the back to make way for the rich, and sometimes unscrupulous worshippers.[16] The feasts released some of their frustrations.

By the time of the Protestant Reformation, the feasts, fools, clowns, and dancing were largely gone from the church. They had been declared satanic by those in power who were tired of being parodied. It could be hypothesized that the suppression of festivity by the Catholic authorities in the fifteenth century, and the resulting solemnity and the growing inequalities of the hierarchy, were contributing causes of the reformation.[17] People simply felt too restricted, and too bottled up. Faith was to be a celebration, not a penance. There is some truth to this, but it is not an uneasy matter to uncover the causes. Luther is reputed to have said, "If you're not allowed to laugh in heaven, then I don't want to go there."[18]

According to Floyd Shaffer, when the Feast of Fools first began, the clown symbol was used by the church both in worship services and in educational classes. The emphasis during worship was on being an interrupter — helping to raise the awareness of the people, much as at the University of Bologna. The clown might be funny in what was being done, but it was always tied in with what was happening in the formal parts of the service. For example, if the people were not singing the praises with enough gusto, the clown would pop up and play cheerleader. Once the interruption was over, the clown returned to the hiding place. 'Clowns sought,' Shaffer says, 'to help people see things for themselves, through exaggeration.'[19]

With new denominations being found every weekend, orthodoxy and heresy became serious matters. Acceptance of the diversity of beliefs within the unity of the gospel was left by the wayside, as each group tried to prove it had the correct understanding of God. The humor of God was no longer a matter to be joked about.

Christians and the Circus

The rage in the 1600s was the emphasis on the intellectual

abilities of humans.. This was especially true as the Puritans gained power in England. Sin was to be overcome by the severity of self-discipline. Pleasure, fun, and distractions were looked down upon. Theaters in England were closed in the mid-1600s. If the Puritans had their way fifty years earlier, Shakespeare would not have written down his plays, and we would not know about him or have his plays today. Think about the cost of this kind of salvation.

No matter. All was not lost. The spark of religious humor remained alive even in this dark time. This century would see the Jesuit Vincent Huby write this litany prayer: "Jesus, crowned by piercing thorns, have mercy on us; Jesus, treated like a joke king, have mercy on us."[20]

By the late 1700s, the puritanical attitudes of England had taken strong root in America. All forms of theatrical entertainment were banned.[21] What humor was left in American churches appeared in sermons and was largely cerebral. It was directed against those ideas and people the pastors believed distracted the congregations' attentions away from complete service to God.[22]

In the last half of the 1800s, a talking clown, Dan Rice, took the religious leaders to task for maintaining this stance of solemnity. He told them there was no sense in trying to "dam up human nature." There was simply "no reason why the Devil should have all the enjoyable things in the world."[23] Yet matters moved slowly. Clowns would not reappear in church until the late 1960s; an absence of 400 years.

CHAPTER 6

Christian Clowning Today

May Christ the Clown work happy havoc in your life!
— Leo Remington

To be a Christian clown is to proclaim that God's power is still decisive in history, that God is still in control. When Christians put on the white face of a clown, they put on the face of death. They die to their former selves, and no longer exist as Mary Bunker or Richard Wagon. They exist only as clowns. It is a moment of conversion, much like the moment when a person dies to him or herself to become a Christian.

White is a universal color of death. Most cultures use it to symbolize human mortality. When clowns put on white-face, they are ageless, sexless, and historyless. They transcend time. They are both male and female. They belong to no race or cultural grouping. They live on the edges of all societies, and are members of all. They cross cultural lines whether society says this is permissible or not. And clowns have no physical needs. They experience no physical pain or pleasure; they cannot even die. Paul's words in Gal 3:28 come to mind: there is no longer male or female, Gentile or Jew, slave or free. All are one together.

After the white mask of death is on, the bright colors are added. The colors symbolize new life. The blues, greens, oranges and reds are filled with emotions and reactions. They speak of the gut-level responses of being human.

The first thing Christian clowns do is to make people laugh. This follows the wisdom of the Sioux Heyhokas. A space must be opened up before the sacred can enter, and laughter does this. It takes down the walls that build up, and heals those areas where we are not open because of fears, hurts, or angers. Since the development of the nuclear bomb, a great deal of laughter has been dampened by the overhanging possibility of death in the next hour. What is more obvious than combating the folly of nuclear war than a good, hearty laugh, and then continuing to work for peace? As Harvey Cox says, "Laughter is hope's final weapon."[1] When we can no longer laugh, we are dead, whether the bomb falls or not.

Not only do Christians need to laugh more, but so does the church. The Body of Christ has its own humors, its own fluids of life, as doctors told us just a century ago. And the fluids must be circulated if the bad humors are not to build up like poisons. When we take parts of our worship service so seriously that they can never be changed, then we need to laugh at our worship forms. When outdated words in our liturgies and doctrines strike us as funny, then we need to laugh at our own faulty attempts to figure God out. And when we find ourselves getting angry when someone presents something funny during worship, then we need to laugh at ourselves for taking ourselves too seriously. Worship involves bringing out entire selves before God. Our solemn sides are not more holy or acceptable to God than our bumbling, error-prone ways. I have to remind myself of this often because I think there is so much at stake. Well, there is a lot at stake. It's our humanity and faith.

There is a time for both solemnity and laughter within worship. The story of Sarah and Abraham should make this clear to us. When Pope John XXIII cracked a few jokes in the 1960s, he shook the Roman Catholic church out of its stupor; at least for a few moments. "The Pope, the one with a direct line to God . . . joking? Incomprehensible!" To laugh is to worship as God worships; with a deep, hearty resounding shout of delight!

Christian clowns also help people feel the range of emotions they feel in their lives. This is not as easy as it sounds. A great many Christians have serious blocks against acknowledging their negative feelings of anger, hostility and hurt. They know something is off, but they don't know what it is because they have repressed these feelings for so long. Others have blocks against enjoying life too much, lest they appear not to be Christian enough, as if being a Christian only involved crossing the finish line, and had nothing to do with the running of the race. One does not cross the finish line and become Christian for life. One has to always work at becoming a better Christian. This is a process.

Clowns are free to experience all emotions. They can feel pain one moment, anger the next, and joy after that, if that is what's there. Clowns have no rules to hold to, no image to maintain. They are everything at once, and paradoxically, nothing.

They can also help people express the emotions they feel. Clowns have no codes of masculinity to prevent crying, or femininity to prevent wanting to knock someone's block off. There are no societal rules that say men cannot care for men, blacks for whites, republicans for democrats, or capitalists for communists. Clowns care for others because they feel like caring. If clowns feel like crying, they do so. If they feel like giggling, they giggle. What clowns feel, they express. They are directly in touch with their reality. Clowns live; they do not spend all their time planning for tomorrow. Joseph McLelland says, "The truly human life is an act of celebration."[2]

A good example of this freedom of expression is found in the character of "Hawkeye" on the TV show "M*A*S*H." The show succeeds largely because of the breadth of Hawkeye's humanity. He is a mixture of skill, caring, childishness at times, and anger at the senseless destruction of war. He is a court jester who dares to see clearly, and speak the truth. Like a clown he takes as serious what others have given up caring about; and as funny what others take as serious. He turns the world upside down, and transforms it into something better. Yet beneath his zaniness and crazy antics, he keeps his humanness intact, and helps those around him to do so in the midst of extreme stress. We admire him, although we do not always agree with everything he does. When a young Marine who is trying to act up to the image of the uniform, says "I'm a Marine; we're the best!" Hawkeye shoots back, "I'm a coward; we're the worst." And effectively two different, yet accepted value systems are confronted against each other, and the viewer has to decide which one to choose.

Clowns challenge us out of luke-warmness to dare to be who we are, and to express what we feel. Their outrageous stunts sneak up on us and, before we know it, we are reacting. Black Elk speaks of this challenging: "When people are already in despair, maybe the laughing is better for them; and when they feel too good and are too sure of being safe, maybe the weeping face is better for them to see."[3]

It does not matter who we are, or what we are about. Clowns accept us where we are, and gently try to move us to where we can be more fully and authentically ourselves. Their childlikeness is so unthreatening that we are invited into their world. Without this acceptance of who we are, as we are, we can never break out of our molds to be fully Christian. We cannot move beyond human rules to integrity.

Clowns not only tease us to the boundary edges of our existence, they also reach in and challenge our core. They penetrate the invisible barriers we set up to protect ourselves and our schedules. Because they are not part of our normal world, we have no set defenses against clowns. We may expect something, but we do not know what. As a result, we are open, and clowns can get in where nothing else can. Clowns will come storming through the back door, and all we can do is watch and listen in amazement as they scamper around our rooms, dumping drawers and pulling out long forgotten memories stuck way back into closets. We experience something unplanned, and hopefully learn from it. But just to be sure our schedules are not disrupted again, we bolt the back door. There is such a thing as too much of a good thing. But the next time the clowns come up from the basement, and we have no idea how they got down there.

Clowns are also prophetic. They call us back to the simplicity of faith, and the directness of childhood. They rekindle the ability to dream, by fuzzying up the line between reality and dreams. We are encouraged to believe we have faith, simply because we want to. Clowns help us see beyond what is limiting to what is limitless. People survive because of their dreams, for when there are no dreams, people shrivel up inside and blow away. They begin to care only about efficiency ratios and production figures. The sparkle in their eyes go out. Why do brightly colored balloons, rainbows, unicorns, fairy tales and elves continue to excite people? Because such things renew people, and help them to dream.

They also love to play with our taboos. Clowns break through the accepted rules to play by new rules; rules without boundaries, and rules that lead to the Kingdom of God. The high places of this world are lowered, and the low places are exalted. The world is turned upside down. Does this sound familiar? It fits the description of the early Christians in *Acts*. Disorder takes over for awhile, and this is good, because it allows us to see outside our rules to new possibilities and to new goals.

Clowns play with our sacred rules, too, and risk being labeled heretics. The danger is real. If clowns simply destroy what is regarded as sacred, just leave it, so to speak, bleeding on the floor; then they have done a disservice and could rightly be charged for the destruction of heresy. What is required for Christian clowns when they work with the sacred, is to bring together something new to replace the old. There must be new sacred symbols to replace the old ones. What is torn down must be built back up.[4] Not to do so is destructive.

Peter Berger sees humor as a signal of the transcendence of rules. He says,

> Transcendence has been, shall we say, declared 'inoperative' by the major agencies that officially define reality — the universities, the school system, the medical system, the communications media, and to some extent, even the courts.[5]

He calls such agencies the "reality police."[6] It is not surprising to say that secular authorities do not care for such matters as transcendence, but it is somewhat disheartening to suggest that often the church does not care either. Too often the church is a structure of tightly-orchestrated rules. The transcendent rarely goes by the rules. One has only to think of Jesus' entrance into this world to illustrate this. The entrance broke the accepted pattern. So did his exit, and his parables, and his life-style, and so on.

The circus is a place that is marginal. It has never been integrated into any culture. Because of this, the circus can seek the truth wherever it is. It does not have to hold matters together. Within the circus, the clowns invert the cultural rules, and bring in disorder. The circus "is a kind of mirror in which the culture is reflected, condensed and at the same time transcended; perhaps the circus seems to stand outside the culture only because it is at its very center."[7] How is the position of the circus important to the church? Substitute "church" for "circus" in the above paragraph.

Not in the Spotlight

Finally, clowns hold a unique position in society. In the circus, clown are seldom the main attraction. They are not the star performers. They move along the sides of the parade, while the main attractions are mounted on the guilded circus wagons. They come out before the circus begins in order to warm the audience up. Then, once the show begins, the clowns appear as fillers between acts, diverting attention away from the preparations being made for the next act. Even at their best moments, clowns in America work only small segments of the audience. Yet, the circus would not be a circus without clowns.

The position of the church in society mirrors the position of the circus in society. Christians mirror the clowns. Because of the nature of their calling, Christians can never be the main acts. They will never be in the majority. At most, they are enablers for other people. Henri Nouwen picked up on this image by comparing those holy women and men in the church who do the everyday tasks to clowns. These are the people who simply lead humble and saintly lives, and seldom receive any recognition. "Of the virtuosi we say, 'How can they do it?' Of the clowns we say, 'They are like us.' The clowns remind us with a tear and a smile that we share the same human weaknesses."[8] There is a danger that Christian clowns may get to like the spotlight, or that clowning may be used as a gimmick within worship services. If this happens, it is time for clowns to disappear for a while.

Clowns at best are unpredictable. At worst they are irrelevant. Yet, can the church have too much irrelevance?

Clowning and the Cross

Floyd Shaffer says the theology of clowning is really the "ancient biblical theology of the cross," and sees four ascending steps in clowning: adoration, rejection, humiliation and crucifixion.[9]

Why are clowns so adorable, so attractive to people? Certainly their outlandish pranks, their image of general happiness, their simplicity, and their directness are all appealing. But what touches us most is the vulnerability of clowns. We have only to look at Charlie Chaplin and Emmett Kelly to recall this. Both of them created characters who try and try, only to fail. Yet they never gave up hope. And they always moved their audiences along to believe in a post-crucifixion awareness.

Most Christians do not move beyond step one in their lives. "Clear across the sweep of the Gospel we hear him (Jesus) promise three things to people who take him seriously: 1. You'll know joy and happiness. 2. People will think you're crazy. 3.You're going to get in trouble."[10] Shaffer continues:

> Throughout too much of the church today we have a lot of
> people who stop at stage one. They want and talk about all the joy

of the Lord and that which Jesus Christ has done for them, and they keep it personal. And that is right and correct. The problem is they have not gone to the second and third steps, which Jesus himself identified . . . If you decide to take seriously the path which Jesus describes in the Sermon on the Mount, you'd better make sure you look good on wood.[11]

Clowns reach the higher steps by being vulnerable. They do not set themselves up as wise or as powerful. In the few cases they do, they will eventually take a fall. Clowns also have no skills to make people "ooh" and "ahh." At best they have only partial skills, which may at first attract attention and admiration, but which always end in the juggled objects crashing to the floor. It is the audience that is set up as powerful and capable.

Another important aspect here is our vulnerability to God. God forgives us only after we acknowledge our foolishness. Clowns help us do this by taking on our sins (absurdities, frailties, hypocrisies) in their clowning skits. Then they absolve them through their laughter at their portrayals, and our realization that we are laughing at ourselves. Clowns take on a crucifixion for our sake, and usher in the resurrection.[12]

Clowns play both images in the Mr. Bojangles dance in the Broadway musical, "Dancing." Mr. Bojangles is old now and cannot dance and leap as he used to be able to do. Yet the spirit within him keeps pushing him to try, no matter how far he falls short. The spirit is represented by another dancer who dances behind Mr. Bojangles. The audience can see the smooth movement of the spirit, and the rough, faltering movements of Bojangles, and the audience feels for the old man. He is striving after something he can no longer reach. Yet the spirit dancer is there to remind him enough that he keeps on trying. Clowns remind us to accept our limitations, and to follow the spirit we feel inside.

The Spirituality of Clowning

The spirituality of the clown is rooted in being an improvisational artist. Make no mistake, clowns are artists; and the arts are one of the greatest channels of authentic prayer. Those who create art and those who enjoy art both feel a deepening of their prayer lives because of the interaction with art. Yet, for artists there is something more than objectively experiencing art. It goes deeper.

The art of an artist is not what is produced, although this is a part of the whole picture. The art is a lived prayer of being an artist. This is a feeling, and a relationship with what has been called the muse, the spirit, the voice, and the God which involves times of presence and times of absence.

While it is clear that artists do use the three major forms of prayer (articulated, meditated, and contemplated) as average people do, it is not so clear that artists place the same emphasis on them. Artists care about the events going on in their communities and in the world; and they have fears and doubts that are vocalized in their public and private prayers. Artists also consciously think out specific concerns, meditating on the inner connections and related problems. But artists dwell mostly in contemplation. This is where their inspiration and guidance comes from. In a real sense, they move in and out of prayer throughout the day, trying to stay in touch with the voice. Contemplative monks do no less. I conclude that most non-artists stop with articulated prayers, although some do meditate, and a rare few contemplate.

The criticism that artists are only inspired now and then could raise doubts that artists walk in contemplation throughout the day. The old formula that says art is 10% inspiration and 90% perspiration, deepens this criticism. Even if the formula is rephrased to read 10% contemplation and 90% meditation, the doubt that artists are in in any real sense praying throughout the day remains. Meditation here refers to working with techniques to codify the inspiration experienced in contemplation. Overall, artists spend more time in contemplation waiting for inspiration to come, and relatively little time on working out the details of how to present the art. This waiting is prayer, even though I doubt many artists, even Christian ones, perceive this as such.

In this contemplative state there is a connectedness with an underlying creative center in the universe.

It is not uncommon to find artists who can never reproduce the brilliance of earlier work, or who have perpetual writer's block. It is not easy to stay close to the center in creating art or prayer. Yet artists will become alcoholics, drug addicts, live in increasingly grungy places, and subject themselves to tremendous pressures in order to be in what I would call a state of contemplation. They want to be able to smell, feel, taste, touch and see life so directly and nakedly that they will do anything in order to do so. Even to the point of destroying themselves. Monks in the desert have done the same.

In one sense, what has been talked about so far is passive artistry. It is still contemplative, for waiting is a part of contemplation. Within all of this is a time of inspiration, the time I call active artistry. More commonly it is known as improvisation, or improv. When artists are inspired, whatever art form they work in, they go with the flow of the inspiration. They do not stop to work out production details, or to figure out how best to present an image. The writer writes down what comes, and goes back later to work the sentences and paragraphs. The dancer lets the reins go slack on the body, and follows it around the floor. The pianist allows the fingers to select the music and the rhythm free of conscious control of the mind.

When artists are inspired, they let go of everything from the past.

Or at least they try to. They release all desires for the moment and for the future, and simply stand naked and responsive before the moment. With improv it is very hard to tell who is receiving and who is directing. The contact between the artist and the spirit is that close. Flora Wuellner terms this a time of "soaking prayer." It is moving into the space where symbols live and take form. It is allowing God to echo within, that one may be completed, transformed, and fulfilled in Christ.

Clowns, as artists, are no different in their use of improv. If anything, they do more of it. They can have the same rigorous background of technical instruction and practice. Yet clowns are known for what they do spontaneously. The nature of clowning is to be as open as possible, and to respond to what situation comes along. For clowns there is no set program, no finished product that can be hung up on a wall to be looked at or preserved. The art of a clown is always in flux, and exists only in the space between the clown and the audience. All the clown can do is prepare as well as possible, walk out in front of the crowd, and hope that something happens. It is a trusting moment. And for Christian clowns, it is a moment of turning everything over to God, to lead, to mold, and to transform.

CHAPTER 7

Itinerant Fools, Clowns, Artists

> All around me were the poorest of the poor — limbless, sick, lonely, abandoned, dying — now being bathed, fed and treated medically by staff and volunteers who offered them respect and love while I wandered about with puppets, harmonica and paper animals. At one level I felt irrelevant; but the staff gently insisted that I continue playing, assuring me that I was healing other wounds, feeding other appetites.
> — Ken Feit, quoted by Patrick Forbes, "Gospel Fool"

Fifteen years after the resurgence began, clowns are found in almost every corner of the church, ministering with their brand of love as no one else can. There are a wide variety of individuals and groups who do everything from acting out the gospel stories during worship services, to visiting shut-ins, to speaking of Christ's love to the world's problems. Some consider themselves artists; some are ordained by their denominations for clown ministry; and some just do it for fun in their spare time. There are a variety of ministries, and a variety of people in them. Here are some of the people, and their ministries.

Nick Weber

Nick Weber is a clown in the old circus tradition. He talks with the audience. This is possible because the circus he works in is his own one-ring show. Actually, he calls it a quarter-ring, and it has the intimacy of a small theater performance. He began his "Royal Lichtenstein Quarter-ring Sidewalk Circus" in 1970, and bills it as the worlds smallest. Weber is a Jesuit priest, and considers the audience his congregation. The advantage of a circus congregation, he says, is that he gets a new congregation every day.

It was out of the concern he had to bring the redemptiveness of humor to ordinary people that he decide to start his ministry. The fables he and his three yearly interns perform are his sermons. Gentle and subtle, one fable tells the story of a miser who did not know the difference between having and enjoying.

The fables are surrounded with the traditional circus acts, although they are often presented on a modified scale. The high-wire act takes place only five feet off the ground; and instead of a number of large horses galloping around the ring with riders doing gymnastics on their backs, there is a small pony who takes a small dog on a ride. Other animal acts in past years have included cats, monkeys, and even a small bear. There is a calliope music, juggling, mime, fire-eating, magic, and lots of humor. The acts change each year as the new crop of interns come with different talents.

The hour-long performance opens with the instructions to 'Take a chance. Throw away the calculated corners of your hearts. Discard your fact-ridden centers of fancy, and welcome the momentary miracle of a smile. Seize this circle until it circles you, and dances you back to the reality of hopes and dreams.' Weber's circus travels around the United States, with many of the bookings being on the lawns of colleges and seminaries. None of the performers get paid, but they do make enough from contributions to pay for food, and for enough gas to get to the next town.[1]

Ken Feit

Feit called himself an "itinerant fool." He had been a Jesuit scholastic for eight years, but after experiencing life in the ghetto, he left the comfortable dimensions of the order to travel the world. He told stories from around the world, created music, played with puppets, and clowned. In him, as in the fools of other times and cultures, the ordinary became extra-ordinary. It was here that Feit felt empires could be dismantled, weapons turned into plowshares, and here that human creativity could restore the balance of play and work.

He saw himself as a fool rather than a clown because he felt the clown was imprisoned by the conventions of the circus; as the priest is also imprisoned by the church. He broke down barriers that separated people through the use of "prophetic imagination"; entering into life's forms and sources of sin pain. He described himself in this way: "a mirror, pattern-breaker, self-transcender, world-inverter; to reveal in momentary chaos and find peace in the worlds of the child, primitive, mystic, artist, and madman."[2]

Once he stayed up all night with a Tibetan abbot discussing the metaphysics and theology of bubbles. He used toilet paper as the priestly stole in his Fool's Liturgy, and celebrated the everyday wonder of a banana, an apple, a handkerchief, needles and thread, scissors and paper, a balloon, and some molding clay.[3] Once he served as Wisconsin's "state fool." When he was in Turkey on one of his annual trips, he hung one of his socks on the tomb of St. Nicholas to see if it would be filled by morning.

Along with Nick Weber, Feit was the focus of a short documentary on Catholic fools. In "Fools for Christ," interviews with the two clowns are interspersed with film of performances. With Feit's death in August 1981, the film provides an invaluable source. Feit was 40 years old when he died in a car accident.[4]

Therapeutic Clowning

Another kind of clown ministry is therapeutic clowning. The organized movement began in 1973 by the Rev. William Peckham, a United Methodist pastor. Today there are more than 3000 of his Holy Fool groups, and over 20,000 clowns working in 48 states and 6 foreign countries. Two churches financially support his ministry: Westminster Presbyterian and First Congregational in Springfield, Illinois.

The emphasis is on-going to hospitals, homes for the aged, psychiatric wards, and drug rehabilitation centers. In these places the clowns try to combat depression, loneliness, and suffering with the healing power of laughter and humor. They do not emphasize performance or shows, but approach people individually. They try to break down the psychological barriers that isolate hurting individuals from caring people. The clowns' painted faces and silent antics often get through the invisible barriers people set up to protect themselves, because clowns are non-threatening and are symbols of goodness, fun, and happiness.[5]

John Towsen says much of the humor used by tribal clowns is intended to be therapeutic. Illness is thought of as caused by demons. One way to get rid of the demons is by comic exorcism.[6] It is as if the physical act of laughing is enough to release the grip of the demons inside. The bad air is cleared out as the person exhales and laughs.

There are countless examples of how therapeutic clowning is helping people. Gracie was an 80 year-old woman living in a home for the aged in Lincoln, Illinois. She was suffering from severe depression, and sat alone in the corner of her room. Nothing anyone did seemed to have an effect on her. Then one day, a 13 year-old girl dressed up as a clown with floppy yellow feet, and bounced into her room. Within minutes Gracie was laughing and showing the young clown pictures of her grandchildren. She hasn't been the same since.

A Presbyterian in Phoenix visits intensive care units as a dancing clown, and brightens the patients' day even without doing anything silly. The clown image is enough to give the people a boost. A 65 year-old nun dresses up to work with geriatric patients at the Mt. Trexler Nursing Unit in Limeport, Pennsylvania.[7] A man in the hospital had not talked for two months, until three high school boys walked in dressed up as clowns.

Dr. Raymond A. Moody, Jr, author of *Laugh After Laugh: The Healing Power of Humor*, considers clowning to be one of the most fascinating uses of humor in healing.[8] Clowning has also worked with the terminally ill. Young people, in particular, find it difficult to talk about their illness, and clowns are good at opening communication up. One boy was unresponsive to anyone, including a puppet troupe, until Carol Young dressed up as "Baby" clown, and pretended to be afraid to enter his room. Immediately he sat up and coaxed her to come in.

Peckham says "Baby" was able to enter not only because Carole was a clown, but also because the boy saw part of himself in "Baby" — shy, withdrawn, and fearful.[9]

Sometimes the clowning is reversed. Elizabeth, a psychotic patient in Minnesota, was afraid to talk with her therapist. Rather than have a clown come in and break the ice, Elizabeth was encouraged to put on the clown's grease paint. She was transformed! She allowed herself to be taken to a local shopping center, and proceeded to talk with everyone, including strangers. Learning that she could meet strangers and be accepted, Elizabeth began to talk and share with the people she knew, including her therapist.[10]

Clowning allows people to back to their childhood and play as they did when they were young. The grease paint acts as a mask. It allows people to hide for a moment, and become another person. Usually this new person does what the hidden person really wants to do, but is afraid to do for a variety of reasons. Then when they discover they can safely do so with the mask, they are often willing to discard it.

Couples often forget to communicate with each other. Frank Mossman, a psychotherapist and a pastor, works with an aspect of clowning he calls "clownseling" and uses it in his counseling setting. He has couples paint clown faces on each other. Often this simple act opens up the care and loving that has been pushed aside for so long.[11]

Julia Williams and Stephen Greiner list three aspects to therapeutic clowning: 1) the participant explores his/her self-awareness of the clown character; 2) the person interacts with the therapeutic clowning enabler or the person doing the clowning; and 3) the participant increases his/her self-esteem and self-worth by clowning. This model consists of the process of becoming, the action of being, and the interaction of belonging.[12] The authors point out that therapeutic clowns are never disruptive, even for a moment in order to set up an affirmation.

Playing with Taboos: Social Action Clowning

Clowns like to poke fun at idols by playing with the taboos of power, wealth, position, and sexuality; all issues that are generally not confronted in daily conversations. They challenge the lofty positions taboos hold over our lives, and seek to restore them to a more proper perspective. An example is the Pueblo Indians playing with sexual taboos.

In the circus, clowns confront the various taboos through skits. The taboos of power and authority are challenged in the clown and cop routines. Sometimes clowns interact with the ringmaster with the same purpose in mind. The taboos of status and security are confronted in the proud and rich versus the poor and humble. Death brings on the skits of delightful terror and the indestructability of clowns.

And sexuality is confronted by role-switching and exaggeration. Charlie Chaplin worked in this area by crossing over and exploring the sensitivity of femaleness.

Circus clowns flaunt enormous, fake genitalia, and parody situations of promiscuity and adultery. Yet clowns never get the "girl" or the "boy" in the end, for that would identify the clown as having a specific sex. Margie Brown explains taboo-playing in this way: clowns "dare to juggle all into the air and let it fall again in a new conclusion."[13] Laughter is one way to break open taboos. "Laughter alone does not respect any taboo," Eugene Ionesco says, "the comic alone is capable of giving us strength to bear the tragedy of existence."

Margie Brown is one of the major Christian clowns in America who works with social action concerns. She says of her ministry, "Mother Teresa took off her shoes to identify with the needs of her people; I put on my clown mask and tease people into looking into their own masks. On opposite sides of the globe, we are sisters in foolishness."[14]

One of the events she participated in was the staging of a clown demonstration before KKK and anti-KKK demonstrations. She describes what happened:

> Last June at a KKK and anti-KKK parallel rally, where a militant confrontation was looming, the event was preceded by a spontaneous clown event. Ninety people of all ages eventually participated, many in clown face, leaving good energy and loving graffitti as they gave way to the next group of serious demonstrators. Play channeled and high emotions of the neighborhood, and the kids drew their own conclusions about how the clown face invites while the Klan mask hides.[15]

It is her feeling that in such matters as protesting war, the clown should be able to poke fun at both the hawks and the doves. Clowns react out of fascination, rather than out of conflict. They want to understand what is going on. They are curious creatures. Yet their juxtaposing of realities usually results in conflicts for others. She warns:

> Myths and theories of "national security," "acceptable levels of torture," Third World "development" measured by the accomplishments of western multi-nationals, become fortressed doctrines, towering over and tantalizing the Don Quixotes . . . The meek shall inherit the earth, not because in them the flame of the human spirit is left flickering. They don't take themselves so seriously.[16]

What is the clown's role in the midst of a revolution, say, in Latin America? Obviously the clown cannot take up weapons and kill people. The antics of the clown are a non-violent form of criticism of the present social order. Yet they at least rival, if not outstrip, the effectiveness of violent responses; and they escape the problems of the greater might being equated with being right. Any assumption of power moves outside the clown's jurisdiction. Basically the revolutionary clown does what clowns have always done — expose hypocrisy, affirm the good things of life that are here, right now, and encourage people to be more human and less inhumane. This is not to say that the person doing the clowning cannot take up arms on his or her own. But as long as the white face is on, that person is in the realm of the transcendent, and this is not a responsibility to take lightly.

As with Russian clowns, clowns in other revolutionary situations are valuable for inspiring weary and disillusioned troops, releasing in-group strife, and for firming up convictions. But if the clowns see hypocrisy on the side of those trying to correct injustice, they will parody the revolutionaries as readily as they would corrupt government leaders. This does not make them friends of the side they were thought to be on. Clowns may take sides, but they never idolize their choice.

The concern of clowns is not just to get there, to the success of the revolution or to the promised land. The concern is how to stay there, where the revolution does not end with the temporary success of this revolution, but continues to push forward without falling into complacency. Clowns never become part of the power structure. They return to those who are still suffering, and fight for a new revolution. Clowns know that revolutions are never over, for no revolution is ever perfect. There is always more work to be done.[17]

Maintaining the revolution involves learning to live on the boundaries, and not just as a temporary resident residing there until the revolution succeeds. It is a life-style, choosing to face hardship, torture, and death in every moment, every day, in order to witness to the vision. Christians are revolutionaries by the nature of their profession of faith. They have died to themselves, that Christ might live in them. Yet the transformation is never simple or complete. To be a Christian is a struggle to be more Christ-like. Sometimes we succeed better than other times; and sometimes we fail miserably. I believe that the presence of clownishness allows Christians to stay on the boundary and sense the coming world.

One thing to remember about the way clowns fight revolutions is that they do not fight power with power, wealth with wealth, or sexuality with sexuality. There is something of a Gandhi in clowns. They like to change the rules and fight on their own turf. Gandhi did not raise an army to fight the British army for the independence of India. He sat down in front of Army trucks and waited. Eventually the British got tired of moving him, and independence was granted. Gandhi called his technique "soul force."

Saul Alinsky provides another example of how effective changing the rules can be. The administrators in Chicago made some decisions that would have made life harder for the poor. Instead of confronting power with power, which the community organizers realized they could not have done effectively, they threatened to fill a fancy civil concert with poor people who had all eaten baked beans for dinner. Their demands were met.

If a clown has a cross burned on his or her lawn by the KKK, the clown does not retaliate by burning something on the lawn of a Klansman. Instead a clown would use the opportunity to roast marshmallows.[18] Suddenly the rules are changed, and the Klan is playing by the clown's rules.

Clowns also reach in and touch the human emotions involved in social events, that they may be tools for Christ's work:

> In another situation, my clown offered a prayer in the midst of a crisis involving the kidnapping and then death of a little girl in my community. During worship in the middle of that uncertain week, I entered and used a baby blanket to portray the complexity of our feelings and confusions. Motherly, I came up the aisle. Proudly, I folded the blanket back to show my child. Panicked, I discovered it empty. Wailing, the blanket covered my face. Dispairing, I wrung it and paced. Raging, I flung it down and stomped in anger. Slowly sinking down, I wiped my tears and those of the congregation, laying the blanket on the altar as I left. Those who hadn't yet cried, cried; who hadn't gotten angry, got angry; who hadn't yet smiled, smiled.[19]

"The power of confrontive clowning is that the audience is invited to make conclusions for themselves, choosing not sides of an issue but a new awareness of themselves."[20]

Liturgical Clowning

The idea of clowning in worship services came about twenty years ago under Rev. Floyd Shaffer. It was not until 1969, however, that he began to use clowning in his parish work. His concern was that worship seemed mechanical. Worship leaders ought to be more concerned with creating an environment for worship.[21] So he began clowning to do just that.

Patrick Collins feels that part of the need to be creative in worship is because liturgies have become too verbal. Missing or under-used are the myths, images, and symbols that allow us to enter into mystery.[22] Jake Empereur says, "We are still trying to celebrate concepts and spoken words rather than events."[23] We need to use our imagination more, our mouths less, and to take more time in creating and planning our services.

One way to bring in imagination is to dramatize the scriptures and parables. Dramatizing allows people to see what the passages look like. This involves a sense other than just hearing. Michael Moynahan, an authority on mime, says drama helps people understand because it is less abstract, less conceptual, and more an experimental method of entering a sacrament or scripture passage.[24] Mime speaks to the heart. It breaks the surface reality, and engages the deeper reality. It makes the invisible visible in scripture.[25]

Other ways of using imagination include having different people speak for each character in the passage; memorizing the text and delivering it was a first-person account; dancing it; or if a musical version of the passage exists, singing it rather than reading it.[26] All of this is part of the re-symbolizing, re-ritualizing, and re-mythologizing that needs to be done continually if worship services are to express what the worshippers are feeling.[27]

After watching a silent clown service done by Dave and Mel Henkelmann, an elderly lady said, "All my life I've been going to worship services that have seemed like a circus. Now I've been to a circus, and for the first time I feel I have worshipped." In the manner of Floyd Shaffer, the Henkelmanns hold the communion bread up to the cross and break it there, and pour the wine by the cross, to make the connection between the Last Supper and the crucifixion more direct and visual. And as a way of closing a communion service, these two Moravian clowns pass out nails to each person in the congregation. As they do so, they take each person's hand, hold it for a moment, look silently into the person's eyes, and then let go of the nail.[28]

Street Clowning

More improvisational then the other kinds of clowning, street clowning usually involves no set plans. In liturgical clowning the clown often sets a specific time in the service in which to interrupt, tell a story, or make a point. Therapeutic clowning approaches cut-off people with the goal of reopening the closed doors of communication. Social Action clowning confronts beliefs and convictions with the aim of revealing how they often don't incorporate the whole picture.

Street clowning means putting on white face and going out to a street corner to see what happens. Sometimes a gag or two is used to get peoples' attention, but most of the time it's waiting to see what happens between you and the people. You react off of each other's actions, and then the reactions. The movement is quickly towards and away, towards and away, as both people play with and try to find the boundaries where they feel safe.

Each year at the University of Wisconsin-Madison, as students come out after registering for classes, "Paninumbo" (Tom Woodward) is there. Using a variety of simple gestures (opening an imaginary door, laying down a red carpet of toilet paper), Paninumbo acts as the only human being the students meet in the whole process that welcomes them to the school.

John Wallace leads groups of people in street clowning. A couple of hours before the time they hit the streets, all the clowns meet to put on make-up, talk about what is going to happen, and then pray that they will be able to convey the Good News to those who will pass by. Then they go to the arranged place, with the permission of the owner if it is a shopping mall, and clown for 30-minute segments. Afterward, everyone gathers again to talk about positive and negative reactions, and to share in a worship service.

The beauty of this kind of clowning is that you can come to people in a short time. The challenge is great, because every person that comes along has different concerns and a different state of mind. The clown has to try to pick up on the hidden and sudden clues, and address the person in just a few seconds. The challenge is also a danger, because some people just want to be left alone. Sometimes even the sight of a happy clown is too much for them. Robert Shields discovered this side in San Francisco when he imitated people walking by on their lunch hours. Some didn't appreciate his skills, and simply wanted to beat him up.

Theological Clowning

Lastly, there is a kind of clowning that involves one's self, but without using whiteface. It is a clowning that is available to all Christians. Every Christian is called to do clownish things, to open all of themself to another person or situation. The theology of clowning is to live from the heart, not from rules.[29] To feel fully, to express freely, to care and love simply because one want to; this is theological clowning at its core.

As you engage in this clowning, you can feel yourself deepening in the areas you risk showing your shallowness. It is the transcendence of God at work. As you listen better, you hear more. As you try to live a more faithe-filled and trusting life, you learn better how to do so. Bearing the message of Christ involves a willingness to become the messate, as well. It is learning to be a vulnerable lover, a servant of others, and a bearer of joy and hope. It is a process of becoming. To be fully Christian is to affirm the clown within each of us and to affirm the folly of the cross as the foundation of Christian belief.

CHAPTER 8

Life as Improv

> What is serious to men is often very trivial to the sight of God.
> What in God might appear to us as 'play' is perhaps what He
> Himself takes most seriously. At any rate, the Lord plays and
> diverts Himself in the garden of His creation, and if we would let go
> of our own obsession with what we think is the meaning of it all, we
> might be able to hear His call and follow Him in His mysterious,
> cosmic dance.
> Thomas Merton, *New Seeds of Contemplation*, p. 296, New Direc-
> tions, 1972

The need for clowns in the church should be obvious by now. If
nothing else, we can use the bright colors and the movement. What is
not so obvious is our need for each church member to be something of
a clown without putting on whiteface. I believe God has a bit of
foolishness reserved for each one of us, if we dare to accept such a gift.

When Christian clowns take off their grease paint, and look like
everyday people again, how do they act? What do they do? I believe
they take with them the insights they gained while being clowns — insights about how God touches people in unexpected ways, insights
about relationships, and insights about themselves and the many-sided
realities of their humanness. I've seen it happen over and over. A normally reserved person puts on whiteface for the first time, and suddenly
goes skipping down the street and passing out balloons to everyone.
That person is never the same again; never so reserved. A discovery
has been made; and like a balloon that is blown up, the person can
never shrink back to where he or she was. They are more for having
put on whiteface. These insights are available for those who have no
desire to be a clown, but who do desire to live whole, balanced lives.

It comes down to improvisation. After the preparations are done,
and it is time to face the people, whether as clowns in a performance or
as people in a relationship, "improv" begins. And while the preparations may be different, the improv is not. Both require the people to be
faced with openness, trust and care. Elizabeth O'Connor, writing out of
her experiences with the Church of the Savior, in Washington D.C.,
speaks of people being the eighth day of creation. God created during
the first six days, and rested on the seventh. What we do with God's
creation is the eighth day. Do we create? Or do we control and
organize what is already here?

Clowns prepare by rehearsing skits, creating costumes, and putting on their make-up. They go out and face the audience, and need to respond to what the audience is offering. They have to respond on the spot. Often the well-prepared skits go right out the window, because the audience has different needs. If the clowns are to touch the hearts and souls of the audience, the clowns must come from their hearts and souls. In this moment of contact, the clowns have to trust the audience to receive what is being offered, and to risk rejection. Both the clowns and the audience have to trust the Spirit to lead and direct the opening up and the receiving.

Being completely open to the moment is the goal of improv, whether a clown is involved, or a person in the pew. Whenever people meet on the street, it is improv; at least it is if any real sharing is to take place. If one person decides before hand that he or she will talk about this, this, and this the next time he or she sees ol' Joe, then Joe doesn't stand a chance of sharing how he's doing. Neither one does, actually. And what they have is a business meeting, complete with agenda, and not a relationship.

The better we are at improvisation in our lives, the better we are at relating with others in meaningful ways. We are open and honest with others. Similarly, as we are more honest and trusting with others, we are also more accepting of our own selves, with all our warts and imperfections.

Improv is a process. It is always going on. We just keep getting better. Some do it by putting on clown's greasepaint. As they become better at improv, they become better clowns. Some join structured improv groups and work on scenarios, relationships and emotions in a neutral setting. Some focus on having an open agenda whenever they meet people. There are many ways to include improv in our everyday lives, many ways to become more who God is calling us to be.

The place where we can be most authentic is the boundary. It is also known as the area of liminality, the area of marginality, the edges of our existence, and being on the threshold between what is and what might be. Here is where most of our growth occurs. Here is where we do not yet see clearly enough to organize our perceptions into rules. It is away from the center of life, activity, and the exercise of power. And although one's reason is needed in order to get here, here is where reason fails and faith begins. The boundary is where we do not yet have convictions, our ethics are blurred, and we are still open to change. Here is where we listen. Paul Tillich called the boundary the only productive place of reflection and perception. If we do not break past the old boundaries to take a leap in faith, then we never grow.

To use a Biblical image, the boundary is a place of pilgrimage, rather than of settlement. It is groping in the dark while listening to a voice we're not sure we heard. It is living on faith. Sarah and Abraham lived on faith when they left the land of Ur. The Israelites lived on faith for 40 years in the wilderness when they were on their pilgrimage. The prophets challenged the settled Israelites to reclaim their pilgrimage past. Jesus' parables take us to this boundary place, and challenge us to join the pilgrimage to find the answers to the questions that he raises. The early Christians lived it; the Christians of the middle age reclaimed it for a while; and today clowns are asking Christians to value it once more. We are called to be pilgrims. This is where the Christian faith blossoms.

Improvisation helps people discover their gifts and possibilities. Growth can be encouraged and problem areas can be reflected on. Practicing in a neutral, and somewhat artificial environment, such as a weekly group, encourages people to try on different behaviors and to play with different emotions. Confidence builds as creativity deepens. With a good leader, personal blocks in matters such as expressing anger constructively and liking one's own body can be confronted and worked through. It may not be easy; but it's far better than blowing one's top or going through life hating one's body. With patient work, one begins to feel that no situation and no person is to be feared because of lack of self-worth. A strong reliance on one's own self develops, along with openness and trust in others.

Improv is a process of healing, opening up, and loving. It's the affirmation that relationships are central in the life of a congregation — that unless the members at least trust each other, nothing else much happens. Daring to be who you are, to be willing to put who you are there for people to see and react to is a risk. But then you no longer have to hide yourself away. If you hide part of yourself, people don't trust the part they are allowed to see. We know who we are in part from how others respond to us. We also know who we are by observing how our body reacts to situations. Often our body knows far more quickly what is going on, and how we are reacting. Meanwhile, our heads are playing different games of denial or rationalization. Improv helps us get in touch with our bodies again.

In a strong sense, God is actualized in the relationships we have. There are no rules. No legalism to hide emotions and thoughts behind, or to tell what we should do. We have only what we are and what we want to do, or we don't enter relationships at all. If we enter also with our brokenness, then Christ may enter with his wholeness. If we enter with only those parts of us that are together, then Christ has no room to heal or guide.

Patricia de Jong has been involved in improv groups for over a decade. She calls improv a "play without a script," and a lifestyle of improv she calls a "life without a script."[1] If we are going to plan our lives out, we're going to miss God's directions and the uniquenesses of people that only appear in the details. To watch carefully, listen closely, and respond spontaneously is what the clown does all the time. They are also the marks of a life of prayer. Think about it.

Improv is a tool that all people can use now and then to break down accumulated artificialities. It is a lifestyle for those who wish to live a life of joy, hope and love. Imagine what a congregation would be like if everyone in it were spontaneous, trusting and compassionate!

The following three stories summarize much of what has been said in this book. They are here because sometimes stories say what facts cannot. The first story deals with how Jesus reacted to those who felt that living by the rules was enough. The second is about accepting ourselves as disciples of Christ even though we have fears or doubts about the whole thing. The third story presents an image of ministering through our weakness.

"The Parable of the Tallest"

In the ninth chapter of Mark, Jesus catches his disciples trying to figure out which one of them was the greatest in the Kingdom of Heaven. This story is about Jesus' answer.

One sunny afternoon as the disciples were walking back to town and joking with each other after a picnic with their teacher, and Philip was telling his old, tired jokes about how many Sadducees it took to change a lightbulb, Barnabas came to the conclusion that he was the tallest of all the disciples. Or so he thought. For as soon as he told the rest about his discovery, they all claimed that they were the tallest.

After all, they had given up just as much as Barnabas had to follow Jesus, so why shouldn't one of them be the tallest? First Rachael claimed she was taller. Then John said he was, pulling himself up to his full height, and cheating a bit by stretching up on his toes. Soon all the disciples were up on their toes standing back to back, and ear to ear and everything else, too — all trying to be taller than the rest. They were so even in height that no one could tell who was the winner. So they called Jesus over and asked him to be the judge.

At first Jesus looked a little disappointed that his disciples should care about such things but, seeing a sermon in the making, he agreed to make the decision. Then, as the disciples all lined up and tried to stretch that last extra inch out of their bodies, Jesus did something un-expected. It seems he was always doing something that no one ex-pected him to do. This time he bent over and picked up the child of one of the women in his group. He set the child on his shoulders, and declared that little Karen was taller than all of them. "But that's unfair," the disciples complained. "That's only because she's on your shoulders, Lord!"

Jesus just smiled and, with little Karen riding high and secure on his shoulders, began to walk the rest of the way back to town.[2]

"Who Me?"

One day Jesus was again out walking on the water, and he asked Peter to step out of the boat and come to him.

"No!" Peter said with resolve.

"What?" Jesus gasped, somewhat surprised, for Peter had never turned him down before.

"I said, 'No'" said Peter again, but this time with less resolve in his voice. "The last time I tried your trick it took me a week to get the water out of my ears, and I picked up a cold I'm still trying to get rid of. So 'No!' I'm staying right here, in the boat where it's warm and dry!"

"Peter," Jesus asked, "Do you love me?"   "That's not fair, Lord." Peter protested.

"Are you going to come out of the boat?"

"But people will see me, and I don't want to make a fool out of myself again!"

"You were listening to me. Was that so bad?"

"No, I guess not."   "Then, Peter, do you love me?"

"You know I do, Lord."

"Then come out of that boat, now!"

"Or what!"

"Or what? Or I'll do my vanishing boat number on you!"

"I'm coming Lord. Don't you move! I'll be right there! I'll be a fool for you! See me coming, Lord? Look at me come! I'm coming, Lord! I may not make it, but I'm coming! Here I come!"

"That's Not Quite Right"

It had been a long day for Timothy. Work had dragged on and on, and rush-hour traffic had been at its worst. But finally, he was *home!* Timothy dragged himself over to his favorite strato-lounger, plopped himself down into the soft cushions that seemed to snuggle the tiredness from his body, and, with his last reserve of energy, pushed off his still-tied shoes, and leaned way, way, back into the chair.

He closed his eyes with a deep, thankful sigh, and was just about to enter paradise, or what passed for paradise on a Thursday evening in the city, when he felt a tugging at his feet. Pushing open one weary eye, Timothy saw Barnabas on the floor, pulling Timothy's socks off. Nearby was a basin of warm water, soap, a washcloth and a towel. "Barnabas," Timothy slowly said, "What are you doing?"

"I'm washing your feet, like Jesus told us to do," Barnabas replied.

"Barnabas, that's not what Jesus meant. Jesus said that only as an example. We're not really supposed to wash people's feet."

"We're not?"

"No. You see, back in Jesus' day people wore sandals and walked around on dusty roads. So a common practice was to wash the feet of guests. It felt good, and it helped the houses stay a lot cleaner. But today the feet are covered by shoes, and we get around in cars, on roads that are paved. So our feet just don't get dirty. What Jesus meant by what he said was that it was to be an *example* of what we should do. Do you understand now, Barnabas?"

"I guess so. But it does feel good, my washing your feet, doesn't it, Timothy?"

"*Oh, Yes!*"

"Is that wrong then, even though you don't have dusty feet? And what about Jesus saying that we shouldn't kill people — that we shouldn't even nurse a grudge against them. Was that only an example, too?"

"That's . . . that's a little more complex, Barnabas. It involves so many factors. One really can't say whether killing is right or wrong."

"Is it also too complex to know if someone is angry with us? And is it so wrong to want to heal the anger? Jesus said if anyone was angry with us that we should . . ."

"Barnabas, I'm tired! Can't we talk about this later?"

"Okay. Ah, Timothy . . . can I annoint your head with oil?"

"Barnabas!"

Notes

Chapter One: God's Love of Laughter, pp. 1-8

1. Rick Bernardo, "Or, As I Lay Laughing," *Evangelion*, Pacific School of Religion, Fall 1981, p. 36.

2. Michael Moynahan, "Discovering God's Gift of Liturgical Humor through Mime," *Modern Liturgy*, December/January 1979, p. 33.

3. Rick Bernardo, "A Serious Meditation on Laughter," *Evangelion*, Pacific School of Religion, Fall 1981, p. 14.

4. Bernardo, "A Serious Meditation," p. 12.

5. Bernardo, "A Serious Meditation," pp. 12-13.

6. Bernardo, "A Serious Meditation," p. 14.

7. Moynahan, "Discovering God's Gift," p. 33.

8. Bernardo, "A Serious Meditation," p. 15.

9. John Saward, *Perfect Fools: Folly for Christ's Sake in Catholic Orthodox Spirituality*, (Oxford: Oxford University Press, 1980), p. 101.

10. Robert Nye, "Laughter is a Serious Subject," *Christian Science Monitor*, September 30, 1975, p. 24.

11. Leo Remington, "Clowns in Liturgy by 'Tug'," *Modern Liturgy*, September/October 1980, p. 45.

12. Emory Sekaquaptewa, "One More Smile for a Hopi Clown," *Parabola*, February 1979, p. 6.

13. Sekaquaptewa, "One More Smile," pp. 8-9.

14. D.M. Dooling, "The Wisdom of the Contrary: A Conversation with Joseph Epes Brown," *Parabola*, February 1979, p. 55.

15. Dooling, "Wisdom of the Contrary," pp. 55-56.

16. John H. Towsen, *Clowns*, (New York: Hawthorn Books, 1976), p. 9.

17. Towsen, *Clowns*, p. 15.

18. Dooling, "Wisdom of the Contrary," p. 57.

19. Dooling, "Wisdom of the Contrary," p. 58.

20. Dooling, "Wisdom of the Contrary," p. 58.

21. Dooling, "Wisdom of the Contrary," p. 59.

22. Ken Feit, "The Priestly Fool," *Angelican Theological Review*, June 1975, pp. 97-108.

23. Conrad Hyers, *The Comic Vision and the Christian Faith*, (New York: Pilgrim Press, 1981), p. 31.

24. William Austin Smith, "The Use of the Comic Spirit in Religion," *The Atlantic Monthly*, August 1911, p. 188.

Chapter Two: Fools and Clowns Throughout History, pp. 9-18

1. Hiler Harzberg, and Arthur Moss, *Slapstick and Dumbell: A Casual Survey of Clowns and Clowning*, (New York: Joseph Lawren, 1924), p. 4.

2. Harzberg and Moss, *Slapstick*, p. 5.

3. "Bring on the Clowns," *Aramco World Magazine*, October 1960.

4. Harzberg and Moss, *Slapstick*, p. 6.

5. Harzberg and Moss, *Slapstick*, p. 7.

6. John H. Towsen, *Clowns*, (New York: Hawthorn Books, Inc., 1976), p. xi.

7. Towsen, *Clowns*, pp. 63-64.

8. Towsen, *Clowns*, p. 59.

9. Towsen, *Clowns*, pp. 59.

10. Joseph C. McLelland, *The Clown and the Crocodile*, (Richmond: John Knox Press, 1970), p. 141.

11. Towsen, *Clowns*, pp. 62.

12. Towsen, *Clowns*, pp. 32.

13. Towsen, *Clowns*, pp. 32.

14. Harzberg and Moss, *Slapstick*, p. 5

15. Harzberg and Moss, *Slapstick*, p. 15.

16. Towsen, *Clowns*, pp. 85.

17. Emmett Kelly, *Clown*, (New York: Prentice-Hall, Inc., 1954), p. 135.

18. "Bring on the Clowns."

19. Floyd Shaffer, "The Clown — Another Fool for Christ's Sake," *Military Chaplain's Review*, (Fort Wadsworth, Staten Island: US Army), p. 20.

20. Shaffer, "The Clown — Another Fool," p. 20.

21. Shaffer, "The Clown — Another Fool," p. 20.

22. Paul Boissae, *Circus and Culture: A Semiotic Approach.* (Bloomington: Indiana University Press, 1976), pp. 164, 166, 167. Boissae deals with the theory behind it all.

23. Kelly, *Clown*, p. 169.

24. Kelly, *Clown*, p. 200.

25. Kelly, *Clown*, p. 125-126.

26. Kevin Bradt, "Body Language Centers of Energy in Keaton and Chaplin," *1981 Clown, Mime, Puppet and Dance Workbook*, p. 2 of this article. Tom Dardis has written a good book about Keaton called *Keaton: The Man Who Wouldn't Lie Down*, (New York: Charles Scribner's Sons, 1979).

27. Bradt, "Body Language," p. 3.

28. Bradt, "Body Language," p. 3.

29. "Charlie," *Arts in Context*, June 1978. Also printed in the *1979 Clown, Mime, Puppet and Dance Workbook*, p. 1 of the article.

30. Bradt, "Body Language," p. 3.
31. Towsen, *Clowns*, p. 342.
32. Towsen, *Clowns*, p. 342.
33. Towsen, *Clowns*, p. 306.
34. Towsen, *Clowns*, p. 308.
35. Towsen, *Clowns*, p. 316.
36. Towsen, *Clowns*, p. 319.
37. Towsen, *Clowns*, p. 342.
38. Towsen, *Clowns*, p. 304.

Chapter Three: Old Testament Clowns, pp. 19-26

1. Leo Rosten, *The Joys of Yiddish*, (New York: Pocket Books, 1968), p. xxii.

2. Fry's comments appeared in *Vogue Magazine*, January 1951, quoted by Crossman, *Raid on the Articulate*, (New York: Harper and Row, 1976), p. 17.

3. Robert McAfee Brown, *Elie Wiesel: Messenger to All Humanity*, (Notre Dame: Univ. of Notre Dame Press, 1983), p. 117.

4. Brown, *Elie Wiesel*, p. 117.

5. Brown, *Elie Wiesel*, p. 119.

6. Rosten, *Joys of Yiddish*, p. xxii.

7. Elie Wiesel, *Souls on Fire*, (New York: Random House, 1972), p. 108.

8. Harzberg and Moss, *Slapstick*, p. 4.

9. Martin Buber, *Tales of the Hasidim: The Early Masters*, (New York: Schocken Books, 1947), p. 26.

10. Margie Brown, "Clowning Du Jour," *Modern Lithurgy*, August 1981, p. 34.

11. Floyd Shaffer, "God Loves Clowns," *The Other Side*, December 1979, pp. 17-18.

12. Shaffer, "God Loves Clowns," p. 18.

13. Frederick Buechner, *Wishful Thinking: A Theological ABC*, New York: Harper and Row, 1973), p. 73.

14. Abraham J. Heschel, *The Prophets: An Introduction*, (New York: Harper and Row, 1962), p. x. The Christian Old Testament scholar, Gerhard von Rad, agrees with this point, in *The Message of the Prophets*, (New York: Harper and Row, 1962), p. 11.

15. Heschel, *The Prophets*, pp. xv, xiii.

16. Buechner, *Wishful Thinking*, pp. 73-74.

17. Shaffer, "God Loves Clowns," pp. 21-22.

18. Shaffer, "God Loves Clowns," pp. 21-22.

19. Paddy Chayefsky wrote a marvelous play, *Gideon*, which brings out much of this humor.

20. Margie Brown, from a conversation.

Chapter Four: New Testament Foolishness, pp. 27-38

1. Conrad Hyers, *The Comic Vision and the Christian Faith*, (New York: Pilgrim Press, 1981), p. 16.

2. Elton Trueblood, *The Humor of Christ*, (New York: Harper and Row, 1964), pp. 10,50.

3. Frederick Buechner, *Alphabet of Grace*, (New York: Seabury Press, 1977), p. 44.

4. Stewart Parker, *Spokesong*, (New York: Samuel French, Inc, 1979, 1980), p. 42. It is a modern Irish play.

5. Doug Adams, "Bringing Biblical Humor to Life in Liturgy," *Modern Liturgy*, December/January 1979, pp. 27-29.

6. Thomas Woodward, personal conversation.

7. Trueblodd, *Humor of Christ*, p. 49.

8. Trueblood, *Humor of Christ*, pp. 102, 103.

9. Doug Adams, "In Forming Liturgies with Parables," *Modern Liturgy*, May 1981, pp. 4,5, & 17.

10. Trueblood, *Humor of Christ*, p. 55.

11. Adams, "Bringing Biblical Humor," pp. 4,5,27,28,29 (esp. 4-5).

12. John Dominic Crossman, *Raid on the Articulate*, p. 93.

13. Adams, "Bringing Biblical Humor," p. 4.

14. Quoted by Adams, "Bringing Biblical Humor," p. 4. CH Dodd discusses this point, saying we have to change the categories of our minds if we are to grasp Jesus' message.

15. Barbara Hineline, an unpublished parable, January 1981, American Baptist Seminary of the West, Berkeley, California.

16. Adams, "Bringing Biblical Humor," p. 4.

17. John Dominic Crossman, *In Parables: The Challenge of the Historical Jesus*, New York: Harper and Row, 1973), pp. 80-81. J. Jeremias also holds to this emphasis on immediate response. See his *Parables of Jesus*, p. 132.

18. Crossman, *In Parables*, p. 82.

19. Trueblood, *Humor of Christ*, p. 19.

20. Adams, "Bringing Biblical Humor," p. 4.

22. John Saward, *Perfect Fools: Folly for Christ's Sake in Catholic and Orthodox Spirituality*, (Oxford: Oxford University Press, 1980), p. 218.

23. Adams, Lectures.

24. Adams, "Bringing Biblical Humor," p. 5.

25. Harvey Cox, *The Feast of Fools*, (New York: Harper and Row, 1969), p. 140; and (Cambridge: Harvard University Press, 1969).

26. Theodore Ziolkowski, *Fictional Transfigurations of Jesus*, Princeton, Princeton University Press, 1972), p. 298.

27. For more information, see Kehl's full article, "The Theology of Clowning," in *Shoddy Pad*, 1978, available from Tom Nankervis, Box

24023, Nashville, TN 37202.

28. Kehl, p. 1. *Shoddy Pad*, 1978. The underlining is mine. John Cobb notes that Paul was one of the first to change the image of Jesus. Paul was not concerned with Jesus as a historical person. He was more interested in the life of Jesus inside a person. Jesus as a human with human feelings was not important to Paul. See Cobb's *Christ in a Pluralistic Age*, (Philadelphia: Westminster Press, 1975), p. 41.

29. Kehl, "Theology of Clowning," *Shoddy Pad*, 1978, p. 1. The underlining is mine.

30. Kehl, "Theology of Clowning," p. 2. Doug Adams points out that "child" and "servant" are the same word in Aramaic.

30. Kehl, "Theology of Clowning," p. 2

31. Saward, *Perfect Fools*, p. 7.

32. Nikos Kazantzakis, *Zorba the Greek*, translated by Carl Wedman, (New York: Simon and Schuster, 1952), p. 151.

33. Kehl, "Theology of Clowning," p. 2.

34. Kehl, "Theology of Clowning," p. 2.

35. Kehl, "Theology of Clowning," pp. 2-3.

36. Kehl, "Theology of Clowning," pp. 2-3.

37. Kehl, "Theology of Clowning," p. 3.

38. Kehl, "Theology of Clowning," p. 3.

39. Ideas from Doug Adams, "Playfulness with Paul's Letters," *Modern Liturgy*, March/April 1982, pp. 4-5.

40. By permission. From Webster's Third New International Dictionary © 1981 by Merrian-Webster Inc., publishers of the Merrian-Webster® Dictionaries. *They note that "fun" is a possible alteration of the Middle English "fonnen" – to fool, make a fool of; and the old French "fonne" – fool.*

Chapter Five: Is There Fun After Paul? pp. 39-44

1. Harzberg, *Slapstick and Dumbell*, p. 9.

2. Towsen, *Clowns*, p. 43.

3. Towsen, *Clowns*, p. 43.

4. Feit, "The Priestly Fool," p. 104.

5. Saward, *Perfect Fools*, p. 12.

6. Thomas Merton, *The Wisdom of the Desert: Sayings from the Desert Fathers of the Fourth Century*, (New York: New Directions, 1960), pp. 34-35.

7. Saward, *Perfect Fools*, pp. 19, 20.

8. Saward, *Perfect Fools*, pp. 97, ix.

9. Saward, *Perfect Fools*, pp. 25, 27, 212.

10. Saward, *Perfect Fools*, p. 81.

11. George Casalis, *Portrait of Karl Barth*, translated and introduced by Robert McAfee Brown, (New York: Doubleday, 1963), p. 3.

12. Saward, *Perfect Fools*, p. 22. The book also includes an important history of Irish fools.

13. Saward, *Perfect Fools*, p. 23.

14. Barbara Swain, *Fools and Folly During the Middle Ages and the Renaissance*, (New York: Columbia University Press, 1932), p. 72.

15. Towsen, *Perfect Fools*, p. 17.

16. Forbes, "Gospel Fool," pp. 3,4. *1981 Clown, Mime, Puppet and Dance Workbook.*

17. Doug Adams, Lectures.

18. Bernardo, "A Serious Meditation," p. 12.

19. Shaffer, "God Loves Clowns," p. 22.

20. Saward, *Perfect Fools*, p. 152.

21. Towsen, *Clowns*, p. 106.

22. Doug Adams, *Humor in the American Pulpit from George Whitefield Through Henry Ward Beecher*, (Austin: The Sharing Company, 1975), p. 7.

Chapter Six: Christian Clowning Today, pp. 45-52

1. Harvey Cox, quoted by Patrick Forbes, "Gospel Fool," p. 11, *1981 Clown Mime, Puppet and Dance Workbook.*

2. Joseph C. McLelland, *The Clown and the Crocodile*, (Richmond: John Knox Press, 1970), p. 152.

3. John G. Neihardt, *Black Elk Speaks*, (New York: Pocket Books, 1959), pp. 159-160. Also quoted by Ken Feit, "Priestly Fool," *Angelican Theo. Review*, p. 1.

4. Crossman would say, 'Parable shatters a world. Myth creates a world.' Clowns need both aspects. *In Parables.*

5. Forbes, "Gospel Fool," p. 2, quoting Berger from Berger's book, *Facing up to Modernity.*

6. Forbes, "Gospel Fool," p. 2.

7. Bouissae, *Circus and Culture*, p. 9.

8. Henri J.M. Nouwen, *Clowning in Rome: Reflections on Solitude, Celibacy, Prayer, and Comtemplation*, (Garden City: Image, 1979), pp. 2-3.

9. Floyd Shaffer, "Faith and Fantasy," *Thesis Theological Cassette*, March 1977, side 2.

10. Shaffer, "Faith and Fantasy."

11. Shaffer, "Faith and Fantasy." Looking good on wood is an image by Daniel Berrigan.

12. Feit, "The Priestly Fool, p. 106.

Chapter Seven: Itinerant Fools, Clowns, Artists, pp. 53-62

1. Some of this information comes from an articale by Robert T. Smith, "The World's Smallest Circus May be Largest Ministry," *Minneapolis Tribune*, March 19, 1980, pp. 1B, 3B.

2. Ken Feit, Personal letter.

3. Conrad Hyers, *Comic Vision*, p. 83.

4. Some of this information comes from "Compassionate Clown Dead in Auto Crash," *National Catholic Reporter*, August 28, 1981.

5. Susan Foster Ambrose, "The Healing Magic of Clowns," *Kiwanis Magazine*, October 1979, p. 27. Also in the *1980 Clown, Mime, Puppet and Dance Workbook*.

6. Towsen, *Clowns*, p. 13.

7. J. Martin Bailey, "Here Come God's Clowns!" *A.D.*, a UCC magazine, February 1982, p. 21.

8. Ambrose, "Healing Magic," p. 27.

9. Ambrose, "Healing Magic," p. 27.

10. Ambrose, "Healing Magic," p. 27, 43.

11. Ambrose, "Healing Magic," p. 43.

12. Julia A. Williams and Stephen G. Greiner, "Therapeutic Clowning as a Treatment Modality," *1980 Clown, Mime, Puppet and Dance Workbook*.

13. Margie Brown, "What Clowns Always Wanted to Know About Sex . . ." *1980 Clown, Mime, Puppet and Dance Workbook*, 3 pages, page 1. In the gospels, Jesus had the sex of a clown.

14. Margie Brown, "Clowning for the Cops," *1980 Clown, Mime, Puppet and Dance Workbook*, p. 1.

15. Margie Brown, "Clowning Du Jour," p. 35.

16. Margie Brown, "Taboo," p. 1.

17. Doug Adams, from a onversation.

18. Doug Adams, from a conversation.

19. Margie Brown, "Taboo," p. 3.

20. Margie Brown, "Taboo," p. 3.

21. Floyd Shaffer, "Fools for Christ, Clowns for Christ," a Faith and Fantasy Ministry Handout.

22. Collins, "Liturgy and Imagination," *The Priest*, November 1979, p. 40.

23. Jake Empereur, "Rite On!" *Modern Liturgy*, September/October 1980, p. 12.

24. Michael Moynahan, "Discovering the Experience of Sacrament Through Mime," *Modern Liturgy*, June/July 1979, p. 6.

25. Michael Moynahan, "Mime and Worship," *1981 Clown, Mime, Puppet and Dance Workbook*, p. 2. Also in *Shoddy Pad*, 1981.

26. Michael Moynahan, "Proclamation," *Modern Liturgy*, December/January 1979, p. 8.

27. Ken Feit, *The Priestly Fool*, p. 97. Hopi clowns do this re-symbolizing and re-mythologizing as a way of keeping their rites flexible and in touch with the people. The Zuni Indians of New Mexico have incorporated such recent things as the moon landing on their religious rites.

28. Mel and Dave Henkelmann, Conversations and Letters, 1981-1982.

29. Tom Niccolls, "The Praise of Folly," column, March 1979, *Calliope* magazine, Clowns of America.

Chapter Eight: Life as Improvisation, pp. 63-69

1. A number of ideas in this section are Pat deJong's. She has a great thesis done for a Master of Arts degree at the Pacific School of Religion: "Improvisation: The Art of Relationship," 1978.

2. The inspiration for this story came from a cartoon by Graham Jeffery, *The Barnabas Bible*, 1976, Mowbray, Oxford, England.

Films

Filmstrips, Audio Cassettes, and Records

"The Art of Phantomime in Church," filmstrip and cassette by Obie Good, about how to visualize the Bible. Aoround $25, available at church supply stores.

"Art of Silence: Pantomimes with Marcel Marceau." 13 films featuring Marceau. By Encyclopedia Brittanica Films, 425 N. Michigan Avenue, Chicago, IL. 7 to 17 minutes each, in color.

"Be a Clown," filmstrip, soundtrack, and reference guide. Deals with basic props, costumes, and actions. Around $23, available at church supply stores. "The Box," 16 minute film, available from Mass Media Ministries.

"Calliope on Parade," record for calliope music, provides a nice background for clowning. Available from Taggert Enterprises.

"Clown Faces," 16mm color film, 30 minutes, from the University of Pittsburg, Hillman Library.

"A Clown is Born," 16mm film by Shaffer's Faith and Fantasy, 15 minutes, color, a parable about being a Christian. Available around $25 rental from church book stores. Also available from Mass Media Ministries, Room 208, 2116 N. Charles Street, Baltimore, MD 21201. Purchase price is $250.

"Clowning for Kids," filmstrip on how to look and act like a clown, for elementary age children. Around $25, from church supply stores.

"Clown for Freedom," about clowning in a repressive regime, starring Martin Sheen, by Paulist Films, 30 minutes.

The Complete Shaffer Clown Ministry Workshop kit, 6 audio-cassettes, includes the Biblical foundation of clown ministry, history of the clown, make-up clues and more. Produced by Dennis Benson, and available from Recycle, PO Box 12811, Pittsburg, PA 15241, or church supply stores at around $45.

Dan Kamin Mime Kit, 6 cassettes, translated into cassettes by Denis Benson. Deals with the history, background, and rudiments of mime. Available $50 from church supply stores.

"Fools for Christ," is a film that combines interviews with Ken Feit and Nick Weber, with segments from their performances. Available from Cathedral Films and many denominational film stores. A list of dealers is available from Religious Film Corporation, Box 4029, Westlake Village, CA 91359.

"Fools for the Lord," 16mm, interprets the Clown, Mime, Puppet and Dance minstry through the 1980 Conference in Ithaca, NY. Available for rent from Glen Palmer, 470 W. 24th, Apt. 3J, New York, NY 10011.

"Gabella: the One True Clown," filmstrip by Jan Mordenski.

"An Introduction to Clown Ministry," filmstrip and cassette featuring loyd Shaffer, on how to use symbolic actions to transform Sunday worship. Available from the Contemporary Drama Service, and church supply stores. Around $25.

"Kally-ope," background music for clowning, available from Taggert Enterprises.

Make-up Training Slides, with Tapes, from Clowns of America, 1315 Blvd, New Haven, CT 06511.

"Mark of the Clown," 1977, 16mm color film, by Faith and Fantasy, depicts a regular Sunday morning worship service, except that the pastor becomes a clown and the congregation eventually joins in. 15 minutes, available from Mass Media Ministries. Rental is $20; purchase is $225. Features Floyd Shaffer.

"Minnie Remembers," 5 minute film, available from Mass Media Ministries.

"Mr. Pascal," 7 minute film, available from Mass Media Ministries.

"Nickelodeon," background music for clowning, available from Taggert Enterprises.

"Parable," 1966. This is the one that got them all started. Shown at the 1966 New York World's Fair by the Council of Churches for New York City. 22 minutes. It depicts Jesus as a circus clown sacrificing himself for others. It is available from most denominational audio-visual centers, and from ECUFILM, 812 12th Avenue S., Nashville, TN 37203.

"Put on a Happy Face," filmstrip for putting on clown make-up, available from Clowns of America.

"That's Life," 16mm by Faith and Fantasy, about Easter, from Mass Media Ministries, 2116 N. Charles Street, Baltimore, MD 21218. About hope, death, and new life. 8 minutes.

"Clown Ministry," by Floyd Shaffer, 4 audio cassettes that pick up where the Complete Floyd Shaffer Clown Ministry Workshop kit left off. Covers theology, stories and Biblical routines. Penne Sewell contributes a cassette on creativity and "unsticking" the imagination. Cost is $31 plus $1.50 postage and handling from Shaffer, 32185 Susilane, Roseville, MI 48066. Also available from Contemporary Drama Service.

People

Doug Adams, who knows an avalnche about humor and faith, is a professor at the Pacific School of Religion seminary, in Berkeley, CA 94709. Street address is 1798 Scenic Avenue.

Jeff Brodsky does clowning for "Bread for the World" in third world countries.

Margie Brown, a United Methodist deaconness, itinerant storytelling clown, also does social-action clowning, and travels around telling her stories of faith. Her home base is 1810 Harvard Blvd, Dayton, OH 45406, 513-278-9286.

Bill Burdick, RD No. 1, Box 459 F, Donnellville Road, Natrona Heights, PA 15065.

Bruce Clanton, School for Sillies, PO Box 13084, Wauwatosa, WI 53212.

Geno Cumeezi, in Chicago, Illinois. With the other memebers of MoMing Community Dance and Arts Center, she had developed MoMing Bozo Clowning technique — a silent, non-performance interaction-oriented, street theater clowning technique. Bozo clowns are trained to become highly-tuned in on their own thoughts and feelings, and the thoughts and feelings of those around them. Silence is maintained from the moment whiteface is applied.

Patricia deJong is a UCC minister currently working at Riverside Church in New York City. She has extensive experience in street theater and improvisation.

Avner Eisenberg, T/24 Dunwooday Trail, NE, Atlanta, GA 30324, 404-233-9091.

Dave and Mel Henkelmann, Moravian clowns, 4353 Malta Street, Philadelphia, PA 19124.

Tim Kehl, UCC pastor at the Orchard Ridge UCC, 5305 Tolman Terrace, Madison, WI 53711, 608-271-6606.

Michael Moynahan, who is deep into mime and liturgical drama, can be reached at St. Ignatius College Prepatory, 2001-37th Avenue, San Francisco, CA 94116, 415-731-7500.

Randall Mullins, pastor and clown, 6008 26th Avenue NE, Seattle, WA 98115.

Thomas Nankervis, Workshop Coordinator for the Clown, Mime, Puppet and Dance Workshop held each year in several parts of the country. Box 24023, Nashville, TN 37202.

Sister Adelaide Ortegel, a clown, puppeteer and dancer, 2939 72nd Court, Apt. 1, Elmwood Park, IL 60635.

Bill Peckham, therapeutic clowning, Holy Fools Group, PO Box 1828, Springfield, IL 62705, 217-753-3939.

Bill Pindar, Therapeutic clowning, 412 Pine St., Philadelphia, PA 19106, a Presbyterian pastor of the 3rd Scots and Mariners Church.

Leonard Pitt has studied classical mime with Decroux in Paris, and masks with Kakul in Bali. He teaches and performs mask and mime. The Leonard Pitt School, 2571 Shattuck Avenue, Berkeley, CA 94704.

Leo Remington, Roman Catholic Priest in the Archdiocese of Portland, Oregon, with the radio and television commission. 2838 E. Burnside, Portland, OR 97214. His home address is 2424 NE 18th, Portland, OR 97212.

Floyd Shaffer, an American Lutheran pastor, connected with Faith and Fantasy, 32185 Susilane, Roseville, MI 48066. His main event is liturgical clowning.

David Tetrault, 110 Richards Road, Williamsburg, VA 23185. He is an Episcopalian pastor whose pastoral charge is the people of the circus. He has done a dissertation called, *The Steeple People Circus: A model for catechesis exploring the spiritual relationships of tent and temple.*

John Wallace, Country Road E. (PO Box 147) Pittsville, WI 54466. He is a clown in the Moravian church, who works in street clowning and liturgical clowning.

Tom Woodward, campus Episcopal priest at the University of Wisconsin, 1001 University Avenue, Madison, WI 53704, 608-257-0688. He does street clowning and therapeutic clowning, especially with disabled people and recovered alcoholics. He has been a clown for a decade.

Religious Clown Organizations

Center for Contemporary Celebration, Sister Adelaide Ortegel, 410 S. Cornell Avenue, Vella Park, IL 60181, 312-834-8352.

Clown, Mime, Puppet and Dance Workshops, Thomas Nankervis, Workshop Codirector, Box 24023, Nashville, TN 37202.

Clown Ministry Cooperative. They have make-up at a discount for churches and clown ministries. They also have a newsletter called *Red Rubber Noses*, and they put out the *Shoddy Pad* series. Connected with the Clown, Mime, Puppet and Dance Workshops.

Faith and Fantasy, Rev. Floyd Shaffer, 32185 Susilane, Roseville, Michigan 38066, 313-294-8563.

Fellowship of Christian Magicians, Box 385, Connersville, Indiana 47331.

Funny Farm Clowns, Inc., Jim Russell, Route 2, Box 170, Butler, Georgia 31006.

Holy Fools Clown Ministry Group, Rev. Bill Pecham, PO Box 1828, Springfield, IL 62705, 217-753-3939.

School for Sillies, Bruce Clanton, has celebratory worship ides built around the church year, for information send a SASE to the School for Sillies, PO Box 13084, Wauwatosa, Wisconsin 53212.

Resources

Bear and Company, Inc, 6 Vista Grande Court, Sante Fe, New Mexico 87501. Newsletter on religious creativity. Feit was featured in the Vol. 1, No. 5, 1981 issue. Subscriptions are available.

Calliope, the monthly magazine of Clowns of America, edited by Bert Sikorsky, 1315 Blvd, New Haven, CT 06511. It has a regular column by Tom Niccolls, called "The Praise of Folly," which frequently has religious themes.

The Circus Clowns. Good supplier for clown materials. They have a catalog, write to 2835 Nicollet Avenue, Minneapolis, MN 55408.

The Clown, Mime, Puppet and Dance Workbook is put out annually for the people who go to the workshops. The workbooks contain something on everything — articles, poems, reflections, up dates, new ministries, and resources. The 1982 book has good information, for example, on how to do the make-up for three kinds of clown faces, lots of skit ideas, and exercises one can do. Often the articles printed in the workbooks have not appeared in print anywhere else. Although the workbooks are for those who attend the conferences, there are usually a few copies left over. Write to Thomas Nankervis, Workshop Co-Director, Box 24023, Nashville, TN 37202.

Clown Chatter magazine, 12100 S. 80th Avenue, Box 323, Palos Park, IL 60464.

Clown Ministry Cooperative; they have make-up at a discount for churches and clown ministries. They also put out the *Red Rubber Noses* newsletter, and the *Shoddy Pad* series. Write to Box 24023, Nashville, TN 37202.

Clownaborations. This is the place that prints Margie Brown's materials — stories, adventures, and guides to groups for clowning. Write to Suite 240, 5055 N. Main Street, Dayton OH 45415.

Clowns of America. Mr. John Tabeling, treasurer. $13 to join, plus $5 for new mwmbers. This is a secular organization that works with circuses in America. Write to 1315 Blvd, New Haven, CT 06511.

Contemporary Drama Service. They have a wide range of resources on dramas, skits, clowning guides. They are in Downers Grove, IL.

ECUFILM. They have a great many films and audio-visual resources for clowns. Write to 812 12th Avenue S, Nashville, TN 37203.

International Mimes and Pantomimes, Route 3, Spring Green, WI, 53588. They have a bi-monthly newsletter (IMP Newsletter) for $6 a year; a bi-annual *Mime Journal* at $7 a year; and the *Mime Directory*, Vol. I on Human Resources (1977) for $5, and Vol. II on Bibliographical Resources (1978) for $5.

Mark II, newsletter linking the loose network of Faith and Fantasy clowns. $6 for 6 issues, from Floyd Shaffer, 31285 Susilane, Roseville, MI 48066.

Mass Media Ministries. They have most of the films on clowning listed earlier in this section. 2116 N. Charles Street, Baltimore, MD 21218.

Mime Directory. Vol. I on Human Resources (1977) for $5; and Vol. II on Bibliographical Resources (1978) for $5. Available from the Int. Mimes and Pantomimes, Route 3, Spring Green, WI, 53588.

Mime Journal, published twice a year, $7 a year, available from the Int. Mimes and Pantomimes, Route 3, Spring Green, WI 53588.

Modern Liturgy magazine. Comes out nine times a year with ideas on how to improve/change/creatively innovate your worship environment. Each issue deals with one theme. For example, "Humor in Liturgy" was the theme of the December/January 1979 issue (6:8); "Liturgical Mime" was the theme of the September/October 1980 issue (7:6); and "Clowning in Liturgy" as the August 1981 issue theme (8:5). Subscriptions are available from the Subscription Department, Resource Publications, 160 E. Virginia St. Suite 280 San Jose, CA 95112. Some back issues can be purchased.

m*Parabola.* A magazine dedicated to the study of myth and tradition. $18 a year, good investment. Write to the Subscription Department, 150 5th Avenue, New York, NY, 10011.

Shoddy Pad. A publication that deals more in depth on one subject each issue that does the *Clown, Mime, Puppet and Dance Workbook.* Of course it's a lot shorter. Done by the same people. Write to Box 24023, Nashville, TN 37202 for more details.

Source Monthly, a resource for mimes, clowns, jugglers and puppeteers. PO Box 453, Times Square Station, New York, NY, 10108.

Taggert Enterprises. They have calliope music on tapes or records. Write to 323 Logan Street, Rockford, IL 61103.

Skits, Dramas, and Exercises

Margie Brown — A seven-part liturgical form that provides the structure for telling the entire Christian story. Found in the 1980 CMPD Workbook. Available from Clownaborations, 5055 N. Main St., Suite 240, Dayton, OH 45415: *A Clown is Born,* a "how to" and "why" of creating your own clown character, $3; *Fools in their Season,* group skits for liturgical seasons, $4; *Good Medicine Shows,* a musical, mime, and masked drama for college-age troupes, $2; and *Good News Caravan,* 8 Bible-story scripts for clowns, $4 plus 50 cents postage.

Ken Feit — "Creative Ministry," 28 pages of how to tell stories, do sound poetry, clowning, mime, puppetry, ritual making, sign language. Its subtitle is "A Magical Booklet of Techniques and Experiences." Available from Celebration: A Creative Worship Service, Kansas City, MO 64141, PO Box 281.

Dave and Mel Henkelmann — "Worship in White Face," 3 pages. A full worship service done by clowns in silence. 1621 Pilgrim Avenue, Bronx, NY 10461.

Janet Litherland — skits and ideas in two of her publications: *The Clown as Minister,* and *The Clown as Minister II.* Both available from

Contemporary Drama Service. "Blessed are the Peacemakers," a one-act play for four clowns. Costs around $15, available from church book services.

Maryene Loeschke — "All About Mime," has 200 skit ideas, and gives some background about miming. About $9, available from church supply stores.

Louis Long — "200 New Ideas, Old Ideas, Funny Ideas for Clowns," found in the 1982 Clown, Mime, Puppet and Dance Workbook.

Wes McVicar — *The Clown Act Omnibus*, 200 workable clown acts, published by Association Press, 1960. Available from church supply stores, and from Contemporary Drama Service, Box 457, Downers Grove, Illinois 60615. About $9.

Jan Mitchell — "Hallelujiah! Amen!," six-clown kit about finding redemption. Available from church supply stores, and from Meriwether, Inc. and Contemporary Drama Service, Box 457, Downers Grove, IL 60615.

Timothy Morrison — "Easter Sunrise Service," 5 pages, from the 1979 Clown, Mime, Puppet and Dance Workbook.

Michael Moynahan — "Bartimaeus," skit, printed in the 1980 Clown, Mime, Puppet and Dance Workbook, 5 pages.

"How Creation Learned to Give Thanks," skit, 6 pages, 1980 Clown, Mime, Puppet and Dance Workbook. *How the World Became Flesh*, a book of 12 story dramas for worship and religious edication. 1981, available from Resource Publications, Inc., 160 E. Virginia St., Suite 290, San Jose, CA 95112. The price is around $10.

"Improv Exercises," 5 pages of 36 exercises, from the 1980 Clown, Mime, Puppet and Dance Workbook.

"Mime Exercises," 6 pages of 45 exercises, in the 1980 *Clown, Mime, Puppet and Dance Workbook.*

Once Upon a Parable, Paulist Press, 1984, a book of dramas for worship.

"Riches and the Kingdom of God," skit, in the September/October 1980 issue of *Modern Liturgy*, p. 9.

David Mura — "Epiphany Mime," *Modern Liturgy*, August 1981, pp. 38-39. Provides a good description of how to present a skit, and provides a script to work with.

Tom Niccolls — "The Flea Circus," how to run an actual flea circus. Found in the 1980 *Clown, Mime, Puppet and Dance Workbook.*

"God's Amazing Love," a youth rally circus program and worship service around the themes of creation and communion. Found in the 1981 *Clown, Mime, Puppet and Dance Workbook.*

"Upside Down Service," 4 pages, with an introduction to clowning, and a script for the parable of the Sower, found in the 1980 *Clown,*

Mime, Puppet and Dance Workbook.

Leo Remington — "Clown Eucharist Service," is laid out step by step, including suggestions for music and directions for clowning. *Modern Liturgy,* September/October 1980, pp. 46-47.

Floyd Shaffer and Penne Sewall. *Clown Ministry,* 1984, Group Books, Box 481, Loveland, CO 80539. $8, with 30 skits.

Worship Service and Program Ideas

Tim Kehl: Adapt a church drama to the medium of clowning.

Show the movie, "The Parable," which depicts Jesus as a clown serving others, and have a discussion of the Christian lifestyle.

Show the movie, "The Mark of the Clown," which depicts a regular Sunday morning worship service except that the pastor becomes a clown, and the congregation eventually joins in. Afterwards have a communion service similar to the one depicted, and give everyone the "mark" of the clown.

Apply clown make-up as a group building exercise, and then visiting a nursing home or such and spread cheer to the residents.

For stunt night at camp or at a youth rally, have participants make-up as clowns and then act out modern versions of the parables and Old Testament stories.

Have a circus night at family camp with each family simulating a different circus act in clown make-up.

Use clown make-up as a way of dramatizing the streotypes and masks people hide behind. Afterwards remove each other's make-up as a symbolic gesture of accepting people as they are.

Have a Children's Day celebration making everyone up as clowns and singing children's songs.

"Getting Started in Clown Ministry," 6 pages is a nice summary of the theology of clowning, program nice ideas and clown make-up. Part of the *Shoddy Pad* series, 1979. Available from Thomas Nankervis, Box 24023, Nashville, TN 37202.

Floyd Shaffer: Make clowning just another program in your church.

Go into hospitals, nursing homes, etc., and share your energy. Clown therapy can also be done if you have some training.

Clown presentations are visual rather than audio, and this is a great help to the deaf and the hearing impaired.

Use clowning for role playing, on marriage enrichment retreats, congregational stewardship programs, evangelism, and so on.

Annotated Bibliography
*indicates an important work for religious clowning

Accurso, Lina. "Faith Plus Humor: a talk with Marie Killilea." *Liguorian*, April 1981, pp. 14-18. How humor helped Killilea cope with the cerebral palsy of her daughter.

Ace. G. "God (Top of my Head)." *Saturday Review/World*, December 18, 1973, p. 8.

*Adams, Doug. "Bringing Biblical Humor to Life in Liturgy," *Modern Liturgy*, December/January 1979, pp. 4-5, 27-29. Good overview to humor in the Gospels.

_____. "Bringing to Life the Humor of Jesus' Miracles," *Modern Liturgy*, Vol. 11, No. 4, pp. 6-7. Points out the acoustical and visual humor in the accounts.

_____. *Humor in the American Pulpit from George Whitefield Through Henry Ward Beecher*. Austin: The Sharing Co, 1975. A study of preaching characteristics, with an eye of the humor contained within.

_____. *Humorous Plays for the Church Year.* Austin: The Sharing Company.

_____. Lectures given at the Pacific School of Religion, Berkeley, California, as a part of his "Humor and Faith" coirse, winter quarter 1982. The course covered humor from the pulpit, drama, the Bible, clowning, art, music, and the theology of humor. The course is taught annually.

_____. "Playfulness with Paul's Letters," *Modern Liturgy*, March/April 1982, pp. 4-5. Introduces the issue's theme, and provides an overview.

_____. "Special Resource: Preaching Jesus' Parables in the 1980s, Vol. 5, No. 1 (A)." *Word and Witness*, pp. 1, 2, 4.

Adams, Doug and Taylor, Margaret. "Humor in Liturgical Music and Dance." *Modern Liturgy*, December/ January 1979, p. 36.

Aichele, George, Jr. *Theology as Comedy: Critical and Theoretical Implications.* Washington D.C.: University Press of America, 1980.

Allen Steve. *Funny People*. New York: Stein and Day, 1981. Deals with seveteen comedians.

Alphonsus Fidelis. "Joy and Religion." *La Salle Catechist*, Autumn 1956, pp. 246-252.

*Ambrose, Susan Foster. "The Healing Magic of Clowns." *Kiwanis Magazine*, October 1979, pp. 26-27, 43. Also in the *1980 Clown, Mime, Puppet and Dance Workbook*. How clowns can penetrate invisible barriers to reach depressed, withdrawn people. A therapeutic tool.

Anderson, David Earle. "Metaphor, Imagination and the New Religious Era." *Liturgy*, May 1976, pp. 142-148. Deals with needing new metaphors to express our religious faith.

Avital, Samuel. *Le Centre Du Silence: Work Book*. Boulder: Aleph-Beith Publishers, 1975.

_____. *Mime Workbook: Le Centre du Silence*. Venice, CA: Wisdom Garden Books, 1977. Founder of the Boulder Mime Theatre, and Le Centre du Silence Workshops. This book evolved out of the workshops, and blends the technique to do mime with spirituality.

B, A.G. "Wit and Wisdom of the Christian Fathers of Egypt." *America*, December 8, 1934, p. 211. (Alfred G. Brickel) A short book review of a book by that title, translated by Ernest Wallis, Oxford University Press, 1934.

Babock, Barbara A., edited with introduction, *The Reversible World: Symbolic Inversion in Art and Society*. Ithaca: Cornell University Press, 1978. Symposium of 1972 meeting of the American Anthropology Association.

Bachman, E. Louis. *Religious Dances in the Christian Church and in Popular Medicine*. London: Allen and Unwin, 1952.

Badawi, M.M. "Medieval Arabic Drama: Ibn Dani yal." *Journal of Arab Literature*, 1982, pp. 83-107.

*Bailey, J. Martin. "Here Come God's Clowns!" *A.d. 1982*, a UCC magazine. February 1982, pp. 21-24. A report of the 1981 Clown, Mime, Puppet and Dance Workshop held in Berkeley, California. It had background information on the beginnings of the recent resurgence of Christian clowning.

Ballantine, Bill. *Clown Alley*. Boston: Little, Brown, 1982. Nice book on secular clowning, but expensive.

Bane, Randall. "The Art of Pantomine in the Church." *Contemporary Drama Service*, 5 pages printed, also on 35 mm filmstrip.

Barclay, Robert. "Christian Sobriety," in the appendix to *Holy Laughter*, ed. by Conrad Hyers. New York: Seabury Press, 1969. From Barclay's *Apology for the True Christian Divinity*, 1676.

Barr, Brown. "Bishop and the Banana Peel: An Inquiry Into the Question; Where Has all the Laughter Gone?" *Christian Century*, July 21-28, pp. 23-27. Nice overview for clowning with youth groups. Contains a report from one workshop using the material.

Bayes, Thomas G. Jr. "Clowning Around in Church." *Baptist Leader*, June 1982, pp. 23-27. A nice overview for clowning with youth groups; contains a report from a workshop that used the material.

Beaumont, Cyril W. *History of the Harlequin*. New York: Arno Press, 1967, rpr of 1926 edition. A general history of Harlequin.

"Becoming Fools for Christ: Clowning as an Aid to Holy Ritual and Service." *Time*, September 1, 1980, pp. 52-53. Nice overview of clowning and the Clown, Mime, Puppet and Dance Workshops.

Behrendt, R. "Laughter Versus Spiritual Gladness." *Benedictine Review*, June 1960, pp. 20-28.

Bell, Joseph N. "Marcel Marceau." *Christian Science Monitor*, December 6, 1973, p. 15. Provides a background on Marceau, with a focus on his role in the film "Shanks."

Benson, John E. "The Divine Sense of Humor." *Dialog*, Summer 1983, pp. 191-197. On why a Christian Theologian without a sense of humor is a contradiction in terms.

Berger, Peter L. "Christian Faith and the Social Comedy," in *Holy Laughter*, ed. by Conrad Hyers, Seabury Press, 1969, pp. 123-133. Provides a perspective from the sociology of religion viewpoint; from his *The Precarious Vision*, Doubleday and Company, 1961.

*Berggrav, Eivind. "Humor and Seriuosness." *Dialog*, Summer 1983, pp. 206-210. Good overview on humor, with a focus on Immanuel Kant.

Bergson, Henri, and Meredith, George. *Comedy*. New York: Doubleday and Company, 1956. pp. 59-190 is Bergson's essay on "Laughter." The book also has Meredith's "An Essay on Comedy," and Wylie Sypher's "The Meaning of Comedy."

*Bernardo, Rick. "*or as I lay laughing." *Evangelion*, Fall 1981, publication of the Community Association of the Pacific School of Religion, Berkeley, CA p. 36. The definitive definition of laughter in one paragraph.

_____. "A Serious Meditation on Laughter." *Evangelion*, Fall 1981, pp. 12-15. A personal reflection on the importance of humor and laughter in daily life, presented with humor.

Berrigan Daniel. *The Dark Night of Resistance.* New York: Doubleday and Company, 1971.

Berson, Misha. "Buster and Billy." *The Monthly,* March 1982, pp. 29-30. On the slapstick in Keaton and Bill Irwin.

_____. "Variations on a Mime: Leonard Pitt's Farewell Performance." *San Francisco Focus,* September 1984, pp. 21-22.

*Bessiere, Gerard. "Humor — A theological Attitude?" in *Theology of Joy,* edited by Metz and Jossua, (New York: Herder and Herder, 1974), pp. 81-95. Good Overview of humor and how it helps us realize that even with our best efforts, we still fall short of God.

Bettelheim, Bruno. *The Uses of Enchantment: The Meaning and Importance of Fairy Tales.* New York: Random House, 1975. Discusses various fairy tales and their meanings for reality.

Bhalraithe, Eoin de. "How Foolish Can You Be: A Review Article." *Cistercian Studies,* 1982, pp. 279-286. An outline of Saward's criteria for discerning Christian foolishness.

Bickford, Raymond L. "Laugh and Live: A Clown's Creed." 1980 *Clown, Mime, Puppet and Dance Workbook,* 1 page.

Billman, Carol. "Grotesque Humor in Medieval Biblical Comedy." *American Benedictine Review,* December 1980, pp. 406-417. A thoughtful presentation of low comedy in English Slaughter plays as a counterfoil to the violence.

Biser, Eugen. "The Scales of the Spirit: Nietzsche's Battle with the Spirit of Gravity." In *Theology of Joy,* edited by Metz and Jossua, (New York: Herder and Herder, 1974). pp. 46-63. Presents Nietzsche's idea of the "free spirit" as the conqueror of too much gravity.

Bishop, George. *The World of Clowns.* Los Angeles: Brooke House, 1976. Good overview, large size pictures, 184 pages.

*Black, Donald W. "laughter." *Journal of the American Medical Association,* December 7, 1984, pp. 2995-2998. Not only does this article go over the physiology of laughter, it also has a 53 item bibliography of medical studies on the subject of laughter.

Blackburn, Tom. "Share Laughs at Own Risk." *National Catholic Reporter,* December 9, 1977, p. 13. Two short book reviews on humor.

Blyth, R.H. "Zen Humour," in *Holy Laughter,* ed. by Conrad Hyers; New York: Seabury Press, 1969, pp. 198-207. From his *Oriental Humour,* Tokyo: Hokuseido Press, 1959.

Boland, Edward G. "Humor's Healing Power." *Homiletic and*

Pastoral Review, March 1984, pp. 53-54. A story about Father Cullen's humor, even as he was dying.

Boll, Heinrich. "About Joy: A Statement on the Subject of this Issue." in *Theology of Joy*, edited by Metz and Jossua, (New York: Herder and Herder, 1974), pp. 153-155. Boll maintains that there must be joyful sexuality in marriage, and not just duty.

_____. *The Clown*. Avon Books, 1965. A story about one person's life as his clowning career comes to an end.

Boonstra, Harry. "Satire in Matthew." *Christianity and Literature*, Summer 1980, pp. 32-45.

Bordo, Susan. "The Cultural Overseer and the Tragic Hero: Comedic and Feminist Perspectives on the Hubris of Philosophy." *Soundings*, Summer 1982, pp. 181-205. The title says it, and the article covers it well.

Bouissae, Paul. *Circus and Culture: A Semiotic Approach*. Bloomington: Indiana University Press, 1976. Chapter IX is on "Clown Performances as Metacultural Texts," which deals with the dynamics of clown skits.

Boyd, Neva. *Handbook of Recreational Games*. New York: Dover Publications, 1975. Of help with therapeutic clowning.

_____. *Hospital and Bedside Games*. Chicago: H.T. Fitz-Simons, Co, 1945. Of help with therapeutic clowning.

Bradt, Kevin. "Body Language Centers of Energy in Keaton and Chaplin." *1981 Clown, Mime, Puppet and Dance Workbook*, 3 pages. Takes a theological look at both of the silent masters.

_____. "Mime as Parable." *1981 Clown, Mime, Puppet and Dance Workbook*, 2 pages.

Branson, Roy. "And Now . . . the Theology of Joy." *Encounter*, Summer 1973, pp. 322-245.

"Bring On the Clowns," *Aramco World Magazine*, October 1960. A quick look at the history of clowns.

Broadbent, R.J. *A History of Pantomime*. New York: Arno Press, 1977; first issued in 1901.

Brooke, Elise. *Theology and Fantasy*. (Butler, WI: Clergy Book Service, 1977). Deals with fantasy and theology as it is present in the works of George MacDonald, C.S. Lewis, Charles Williams, and J.R.R. Tolkien.

*Brown, Joseph Epes. Conversation with D.M. Dooling, recorded in "The Wisdom of the Contrary: A Conversation with Joseph Epes Brown." *Parabola*, February 1979, pp. 54-65. Talks about Black Elk and Sioux Heyhokas who merge religious leadership with tribal clown-ing.

Brown, Margie. "A Clown is Born." *Clownaborations*. A "how-to" and "why" of creating your own clown character.

*_____. "Clowning du Jour and other Entries for Foolish Feasting." *Modern Liturgy*, August 1981, pp. 34-35, 21. Speaks about what Christian clowning is, especially in regards to play-ing with social taboos. Clowns are wholeness.

_____. "Clowning for the Cops." *1980 Clown, Mime, Puppet and Dance Workbook*, 3 pages. Con fronting the political and technological world by clowning. Her encounter with cops in Geneva is told.

_____. "Fools in their Season." *Clownaborations*. Group skits for liturgical seasons.

_____. "Good Medicine Shows." *Clownaborations*. A musical, mime, and masked drama for college-age troupes.

_____. *The Good News Caravan*, Clownaborations, 1979, rev. 1981. Stories for telling, 8 Bible-story scripts for clowns.

*_____. "Rehearsal in the Center Ring: An Ap-proach to Clown Liturgy." *1980 Clown, Mime, Puppet and Dance Workbook*, 3 pages. Contains her seven-part liturgical form that deals with birth, confession, forgiveness, teaching, crucifixion, silence, and resurrection.

_____. *Stick Stories*. San Jose: Resource Publica-tions. More Stories.

_____. "Taboo or Not Taboo: That is the Question." *1981 Clown, Mime, Puppet and Dance Workbook*. 3 pages. How clowns make fun of everybody, choose new awareness rather than sides, and how clowns stretch definitions.

*_____. "What Clowns Always Wanted to Know About Sex." *1980 Clown, Mime, Puppet and Dance Work book*, 3 pages. Much of it is on sexuality, and how age-old questions that were once responded to by monastic vows, are now being responded to with economic justice, human dignity, and political freedom.

Brown, Norman O. "Person." from *Love's Body*.

*Brown, Robert McAfee. *The Collect'd Writings of St. Hereticus*. Philadelphia: Westminster Press, 1964. The two Hereticus books do an excellent job of having fun with words and with the forms of everyday faith.

_____. *Creative Dislocation – The Movement of Grace*. Nashville: Abingdon Press, 1980. One book in the Journeys of Faith series, edited by Robert Raines. This one tells the story of Brown and how responding to the unexpected has formed his life.

_____. *Elie Wiesel Messenger to All Humanity*. Notre Dame: University of Notre Dame Press, 1983.

*_____. *The Hereticus Papers: Volume II of the Collect'd Writings of St. Hereticus*. Philadelphia: Westminster Press, 1979.

_____. "Saint Hereticus: E. Pluribus Marty." *Christianity and Crisis*, April 3, 1978, pp. 76-77.

_____. "The Spirit's Eighth Gift." *Christianity and Crisis*, February 4, 1980, pp. 8-10.

_____. *Theology in a New Key: Responding to Liberation Themes*. Philadelphia: Westminster Press, 1978.

_____. *Unexpected News: Reading the Bible with Third World Eyes*. Philadelphia: Westminster Press, 1984. A good book for looking at the Bible with eyes cleared of some preconceptions; important for finding the original intent of the passages.

Bruce, Lenny. *The Essential Lenny Bruce*. John Cohen, ed. New York: Ballantine Books, 1967. No nonsense observations delivered straight from the hip. The sharpness of eye is a lesson for clowns.

Buber, Martin. *Tales of the Hasidim: The Early Masters*. New York: Schocken Books, 1947.

Buechner, Frederick. *The Alphabet of Grace*. New York: Seabury Press, 1977.

_____. *The Book of Bebb*. New York: Atheneum, 1979. Four novels together, filled with images for clowning.

*_____. *Peculiar Treasures: A Biblical Who's Who*. New York: Harper and Row, 1979. Wonderful portraits of the Motley crew that makes up the Bible.

*_____. *Telling the Truth: The Gospel as Tragedy, Comedy, and Fairy Tale*. New York: Harper and Row, 1977. An important book; approaches the Christian faith from these three major viewpoints; and synthesizes a final outlook. Dynamic.

*_____. *Wishful Thinking: A Theological ABC*. New York: Harper and Row, 1973. Buechner has a knack for retelling the old stories and traditions of Christianity in fresh and re-challenging ways.

Bunker, J. "Pun." *Sign*, October 1936, pp. 178-179.

Burgess, Hovey. *Circus Techniques*. Thomas Crowell, 1977. 150 stunt techniques centering around balance and vaulting.

Burke, William. "Send in the Clowns." *Modern Liturgy*, September/October 1980, p. 15.

Burt, Jesse. "Rediscovering the Light Touch." *Religion in Life*, Summer 1976, pp. 233-237.

Buscaglia, Leo. *Love*, Bantam Books. Good for use in therapeutic clowning: hands on stuff.

Bushnell, Horace. "Work and Play," from *Work and Play*. New York: Charles Scribner, 1864.

C, P.J. "Laughter." *Ave Maria*, October 24, 1936, p. 533.

Campbell, Patricia. *Passing the Hat*. New York: Delacorte, 1981. A good survey of street performers in America today.

Canonization of a Humorist." *Catholic World*, June 1935, pp. 257-262. "The highest vocation is that fo the priest, next is that of the humorist." Good presentation on St. Thomas More and his constant stream of jokes and witticisms.

Cardenal, Ernesto. "The Gospel in Solantiname." in *Theology of Joy*, edited by Metz and Jossua. New York: Herder and Hereder, 1977, pp. 107-112. A selection from the *Gospel in Solantiname*; about the meaning of Jesus' birth in a revolutionary situation.

Carlo. *The Juggling Book*. New York: Random House, 1974. An okay primer for beginning.

Cary, Steven B.B. *Juggling the Old Testament*. Berkeley: Leonardo Press, 1982. A pictorial volume on how to tell the entire history of the Old Testament, with its 762 major characters, through the medium of juggling. Quite the unique approach.

Casalis, George. *Portrait of Karl Barth*. Translated and introduced by Robert McAfee Brown. New York: Doubleday and Co., 1963.

Casselberry, Diane. "Clowning Around Hones the Language of Pantomime." *Christian Science Monitor*. About Peggy Williams, a clown for Ringling Brothers and Barnum and Bailey Circus.

Chandler, Charlotte. *Hello, I Must be Going: Groucho and his Friends*. Garden City: Doubleday and Co., 1978.

Chandler, Russ. "Does the Door Rate a '10'?" *The Wittenburg Door*, June-July 1981, pp. 3, 6-9, 16. An interview with the staff about what they are trying to do with their humor in the Christian Church. A slightly bizarre, yet hilarious publication.

Chaplin, Charles. *My Autobiography.* New York: Simon and Schuster, 1964. A good book to start with in understanding Chaplin.

"Charlie." *Arts in Context,* June 1978. Also printed in the *1979 Clown, Mime, Puppet and Dance Work-book,* 1 page. A brief reflection on Charlie Chaplin.

Chesterton, G.K. "Where is the Joke?" *G.K.'s Weekly,* March 28, 1935, p. 37.

Christensen, Duane L. "Anticipatory Paronomasia in Jonah 3: 7-8 and Genesis 37:2." *Revue Biblique,* April 1983, pp. 261-263. A Hebrew word study.

Christianity Today. "Religious Cartoons: Needling Inconsistencies." *Christianity Today,* pp. 39-40.

Clanton, Bruce. "Imaging: Laughter." *Mdern Liturgy,* September/October 1980, p. 16. A listing of humorous books to read.

_____. "Masks." *1980 Clown, Mime, Puppet and Dance Workbook.* A starter introduction for germinating thoughts about masks and faces.

Cline, Paul. *Fools, Clowns and Jesters.* La Jolla: Green Tiger Press, 1983, 58 pages. Large-sized book made up of quotes and colorful drawings of various historical figures. A nice collector's item.

"Clowning Around." *Group Magazine,* December 1979.

"Clowns and Round Things." *Church Teachers Magazine,* Spring 1982.

"A Clown's Checklist." *1981 Clown, Mime, Puppet andDance Workbook,* 2 pages. Details of make-up, and props for worship and the workshop.

Colette, Jacques. "Joy, Pleasure and Anguish — Thoughts on Barth and Mozart." in *Theology of Joy,* edited by Metz and Jossua. New York: Herder and Herder, 1974, pp. 96-104. Starts with Barth's devotion to Mozart, and moves on to deal with the theology in Mozart's work.

Collins, Patrick W. "Liturgy and Imagination: The Next Phase of Renewal?" *The Priest,* November 1979, pp. 40-44. How the use of stories and imagination can create space for worshippers to walk around in and find their place.

_____. More than Meets the Eye. Ramsey, NJ: Paulist Press, 1983. Solid book on the connections between imagination, liturgy, art, and, ritual.

_____. "Music: A Parable of Ritual." *Modern Liturgy*, April 1983, pp. 4-5, 16-17. Explores the dimensions of creation and participation in musical events.

_____. "Remembering Into the Future: 1973-1983." *Modern Liturgy*, February 1984, pp. 2, 8-9. On the nature of human ritual.

*_____. "Ritual as a Way to Peace." *Modern Liturgy*, September 1984, pp. 10-12. Moving the rituals of renewal in worship into rituals of renewal in society.

Conn, Harvie M. "Please Pray for Woody Allen." *Christianity Today*, November 6, 1981, pp. 90-91. When comedy moves from myth into reality, we no longer laugh.

Cooney, Randy. "Mime: the Body Language of Proclamation." *Modern Liturgy*, 6:1, p. 8.

Corbett, Jan. "When Fools Rush In." *Today's American Baptist*, October 1981, pp. 8-10. About miming in worship, with a focus on the Fools Rush In Mime Troupe.

Cormier, Henri. *The Humor of Jesus*. Canfield, OH: Alba House.

Corrigan, Robert W, edited and introduced. *Comedy: Meaning and Form*. San Francisco: Chandler Press, 1965. Lectures on comedy and the comic.

Cousins, Norman. *Anatomy of an Illness*. New York: Bantam, 1981. The story of a man who laughed himself back to health, and the reluctance of the medical profession to believe laughter was a big part of the recovery.

*Cox, Harvey. *The Feast of Fools: A Theological Essay on Festivity and Fantasy*. New York: Harper and Row, 1969. Sets a theological basis for bringing festivity and fantasy back into Church. Chapter 10 on "Christ the Harlequin" is particularly good.

Cox, Roger L. "Invented Self; an Essay on Comedy." *Soundings*, Summer 1974, pp. 139-156.

Coxe, Anthony Hippisley. *A Seat at the Circus*, rev. ed. Hamden, CT: Archon Books, 1980. Chapter 14 is on clowns, as iconotects and iconoclasts.

Croft-Cooke, Rupert, and Cotes, Peter. *Circus: A World History*. New York: Macmillan Publishing Co, 1977. Chapter 6 deals with clowns, and has large color pictures.

Crossan, John Dominic. *Cliffs of Fall: Paradox and Polyvalence in the Parables of Jesus.* New York: Seabury Press, 1980. Continues the discussion started in *In Parables.*

_____. *The Dark Interval: Towards a Theology of Story.* Niles, IL: Argus Communications, 1975.

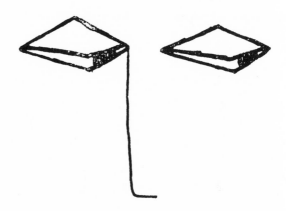

*_____. *In Parables: The Challenge of the Historical Jesus.* New York: Harper and Row, 1973. Looks at the parables of Jesus from the theological and literary approaches; discusses the importance of understanding metaphor.

*_____. *Raid on the Articulate: Cosmic Eschatology in Jesus and Borges.* New York: Harper and Row, 1976. Details how Jesus and Jorge Luis Borges play with and break language and language forms to reveal new insights; shows how literary criticism is as valuable as historical criticism as a tool for doing biblical exegesis, especially in the face of so much oral tradition in ancient Israel.

Crowther, Carol. *Clowns and Clowning.* MacDonald, 1978.

Crumrine, N. Ross. "Capakuba, the Mayo Easter Ceremonial Impersonator: Explanations of Ritual Clowning." *Journal for the Scientific Study of Religion,* Spring 1969, pp. 1-22. On the use of masks and impersonation during Lenten services.

Crumrine, N. Ross, and Halpin, Marjorie. *The Power of Symbols: Masks and Masquerade in the Americas.* Vancouver, BC: University of British Columbia Press, 1983. Papers delivered at the 42nd International Congress of the Americanists.

Culhane, John. "Unforgettable Emmett Kelley." *Reader's Digest,* December 1979, pp. 134-138. A personal reflection on the circus clown who never gave up hope.

Cummings, e.e. "One Winter Afternoon." *1980 Clown, Mime, Puppet and Dance Workbook.* A good poem about encountering a clown.

Danker, Frederick W. "Laughing with God." *Christianity Today,* January 6, 1967, pp. 16-17.

Dardis, Tom. *Keaton: The Man Who Wouldn't Lie Down.* New York: Charles Scribner's Sons, 1979. A biography, with pictures!

Dauphin Way United Methodist Church. "Clowns Against Frowns." *1980 Clown, Mime, Puppet and Dance Workbook,* 2 pages. A local church ministry program, with beginning ideas about clowning, and basic clown types.

Davenport, Demorest. "I Am Not What I Seem!" *Parabola,* Summer 1981, pp. 32-39. Deals with masks in the animal world.

Davenport, Gary. "Eliot's 'The Cocktail Party': Comic Perspectives as Salvation." *Modern Drama,* September 1974, pp. 301-306.

Davis, Ron G. *The San Francisco Mime Troupe: the First 10 Years.* Palo Alto: Ramparts Press, 1975.

DeAngelis, William. *Acting Out the Gospels with Mimes, Puppets, and Clowns*, Twenty-third Publications, 1982. Skits with helpful directions.

Deck, Allan Figueroa. "Liturgy and Mexican American Culture." *Modern Liturgy*, October 1976, pp. 24-26.

Decroux, Etienne. *Paroles sur le Mime*. Paris: Gallimard, 1963.

_____. *Words on Mime*. New York: Drama Book Publishers.

_____. Article by Eric Bentley, "Each Art Has Its Own Territory." in *Mimes on Miming*, ed. by Bari Rolfe, pp. 106-107.

*DeJong, Patricia. *Improvisation: The Art of Relationship (The Story of Happenstance, a Campus Ministry Improvisational Theater Troupe)*. M.A. Thesis, 1978, Pacific School of Religion, Berkeley, California. A great piece on improvisation, as seen with the eyes of someone in an on-going group.

Delaney, Hubert. "Immortal Diamond: the Possible Dream." *Religious Studies*, June 1983, pp. 143-159. Play as a way of re-affirming belief in God.

DePaola, Tomie. *The Clown of God*, Harcourt Brace Jovanovich.

De Vries, Calvin. "Peter DeVries: The Vale of Laughter." *Theology Today*, April 1975, pp. 10-20.

Dialog Magazine. The Summer 1983 issue is devoted to Humor and Laughter. With articles by Eivind Berggrav, Eric Gritsh, Conrad Hyers, Harris Kaasa, Robert Levy, Lorenz Nieting, and John Vannorsdall.

Dillenberger, John. "Visual Arts: the Discipline of Seeing." *Modern Liturgy*, December/January 1979, pp. 34-35.

Directions. "Companies of Holy Fool." ABC Television, August 26, 1979. Interviews and performances by Bill Peckham (clowning), Nancy and John Sipes (mimes), and Betsy Brown (puppets).

Disher, M. Wison. *Clowns and Pantomimes*. 1925. Reissued by Benjamin Blom, New York and London, 1968. A classical treatment of clown origins.

Donnelly, F.P. "Humor: a Denatured Fallacy." *Thought*, September 1934, pp. 286-295.

*Dooling, D.M. "Focus." *Parabola*, Summer 1981, pp. 2-3. A nice introduction to the issues on masks and metaphor. The mask is always greater than one's self.

* _____. "The Wisdom of the Contrary: A Conversation with Joseph Epes Brown." *Parabola*, February 1979. Excellent dis-

cussion with Brown about Black Elk and the Sioux Heyhokas who merge religious leadership with tribal clowning; how laughter opens up sacred space.

Dorcey, Jean. *Mime: Decroux, Barrault, Marceau.* New York: R. Speller Company, 1961. On the 20th century French revival of mime.

Duddington, John W. "Conclusive Laughter of God (raising of Jairus' daughter)". *Christianity and Literature*, Summer 1982, pp. 19-31.

Dunn, Robert. "Discriminations in the Comic Spirit in the Story of Susanna," *Christianity and Literature*, Summer 1982, pp. 19-31.

Durken, Daniel. "Let's Laugh a Little." *Priest*, May 1971, pp. 31-36. A nice presentation for laughter in church matters. Presents St. Peters as the greatest of New Testament clowns.

Dvorchak, Bob. "Clown Minister Comforts Needy." *The Daily Review*, Hayward, California, February 10, 1983. Good article on Bill Pandar's therapeutic clown ministry.

Edenborough, Susan. "Humor in Liturgical Banners and Visuals." *Modern Liturgy*, December/January 1979, p. 37.

Eliade, Mircea. *Myths, Rites, Symbols: A Mircea Eliade Reader.* Edited by Beane and Doty. New York: Harper and Row, 1975, two volumes. Deals with the functions and connections of myths, rites and symbols.

Empereur, Jake. "The Acculturation of the Liturgy." *Modern Liturgy*, October 1976, pp. 8-10. On the need for experimentation in liturgy.

——————————. "Rite On!" *Modern Liturgy*, September/October, 1980, pp. 12, 22-23. About how liturgy has become too verbal, and needs to provide more space for imagination; liturgical uses of mime.

——————————. "Rite On!" *Modern Liturgy*, August 1981, p. 10. On liturgical clowning.

——————————. "Rite On!" *Modern Liturgy*, March 1983, pp. 12, 29. On storytelling as a liturgical form.

*——————————. "The Theological Experience." *Chicago Studies*, Spring 1977, pp. 462. Dives deep into models of liturgical theology; talks about liminality and pluralism.

——————————. "With Liturgy and Justice for All." *Modern Liturgy*, September 1984, pp. 16-17.

Erasmus, Desiderius. *The Praise of Folly*, translated by Hoyt

Hudson. Princeton: Princeton University Press, 1970. Satire against the Church of his day; and for Paul's folly of the cross.

Faber, Heije. "Second Thoughts on the Minister as Clown." *Pastoral Psychology*, Winter 1979, pp. 132-137. Uses the model of a clown to talk about minstry, and how aspects of clowning should be a part of the ministry for all pastors.

Farrel, Michael J. "Does God Have a Sense of Humor?: The Critic's Cartoonists Thought So." *National Catholic Reporter*, June 20, 1980, pp. 14-15. Introduction to the book of cartoons, *Pilgrim's Regress*.

Fedotov, G.P. *The Russian Mind.* Cambriged: Harvard University Press, 1966. Pages 316-343 are on holy fools.

Feeney, J. "The Laughter of Christ." *Revue de l'Universite d'Ottawa*, October-December 1965, pp. 237-253.

Feit, Ken. "The Cosmic Fool Haikus." *Bear and Company,* Vol. 1, No. 5, p. 7.

*_____. "Creative Ministry: A Magical Booklet of Techniques and Experiences." Kansas City: Calebration, A Creative Worship Service. 28 pages. Great resource! Deals with story-telling, puppetry, sign language, mime, clowning, music, ritual making, and sound poetry.

*_____. Eulogy by Fox and others. In *Bear and Company*, the little magazine, Vol. I, No. 5, 1981. Personal remembrances by people who were close to Feit.

*_____. 1978 Friend's letter. Six pages about his trip to Africa: thoughts, meditations, insights.

*_____. 1979 Friend's letter. Ten pages about his trip to India, Nepal, Sri Lanka; thoughts and insights.

*_____. 1980 Friend's letter. Six pages about his personal spiritual journey, written upon the occasion of his 40th birthday.

*_____. 1981 Friend's letter. Twenty-two pages about his thoughts and experiences on his trip to the Middle East.

*_____. "How Many Provincials Have Their Phones Bugged?" in *The New Jesuits*, by G. Riemer. Boston: Little, Brown, 1971, pp. 299-332. Excellent interview with Feit about his vision for the Jesuits, the Church, and the world; done when he was 30 years old.

*_____. "In Praise of Hands." *Liturgy*, January 1976, pp. 6-18. A look at physical language as expressed through hands; especially in deaf sign and Indian sign; with ideas for developing your own sign language.

_____. "The Milwaukee Police Department: An In-Depth Study." Council on Urban Life in Milwaukee, Wisconsin, April 1970.

*_____. Personal letter, October 5th. 1 page. Talks about how he seems himself, and what his message is.

*_____. "The Priestly Fool." *Anglican Theological Review*, June 1975, pp. 97-108. Overview of fools in different cultures; and stresses the need to be continually resymbolizing, reritualizing, and remythologizing for the community. This is the only material I have found that Feit wrote for the mass media.

*_____. "Reflections of a Sound Poet." *Liturgy*, May 1976, pp. 149-154. On having words sound like the essence of the objects they point to. Also deals with why cats purr differently in different countries. Includes exercises for creating your own sounds and words.

_____. "St. Louis Area Jesuits and the Inter-racial Apostolate, 1823-1969," a study of Jesuit-owned slaves in Missouri, 1969.

*_____. "Storytelling." (article) *Liturgy*, March 1973, pp. 16-17. On the role of the story-teller, with ideas on how to begin telling your own.

*_____. "Storytelling." (column) *Liturgy*, August/September 1976, pp. 215, 217. His introductory column about the spider of his life, and telling one's own story.

*_____. "Storytelling." (column) *Liturgy*, October 1976, p. 249. On recording stories children tell.

*_____. "Storytelling." (column) *Liturgy*, December 1976, pp. 320-321. Examples of stories from various cultures, plus hints on how to get a story going.

_____, with Fox, Matthew. "The Storyteller as Prophet." *Bear and Company*, Vol. 1, No. 5, pp. 6-7.

_____, with Richard Zipfel, SJ. "The American Resistance and the American Church, "a study from the late 1960s.

*_____. (About Feit) "Compassionate Clown Dead in Auto Crash." *National Catholic Reporter*, August 28, 1981.

*_____. (About Feit) by Matthew Fox. "A Eulogy Remembering Ken Feit and Other Cosmic Fools." *Bear and Company*, Vol. 1, No. 5, pp. 2-5. Excellent summary of Feit and his ministry.

*_____. (About Feit) by Matthew Fox. "Transcendence and More: About Ken Feit." *Bear and Company*, Vol. 1, No. 5, pp. 8-9. Short remembrances of Ken by some who knew him.

_____. (About Feit) by Mary Aileen Schmiel. "Holidays and Wholly Dazed." *Bear and Company*, Vol. 1, No. 5, p. 10. Involves Ken Feit.

_____. (About Feit) by Mary Aileen Schmiel. "Praymate of the Month." *Bear and Company*, Vol. 1, No. 5, pp. 11-12. A nice treatment of Ken and his life.

Fellini, Federico. *Fellini on Fellini.* London: Methuen, 1976, edited by Anna Keel and Christian Stritch.

Fields, W.C. *W.C. Fields by Himself: His Intended Autobiography.* Englewood Cliffs: Prentice-Hall, 1973.

Fincher, Jack. "Robert Shields: Mime in the Streets." in *Mimes on Miming*, ed. by Bari Rolfe, pp. 211-215. Re-print of a *Saturday Review* article, August 12, 1972.

Findlater, Richard. *Joe Grimaldi: His Life and Theatre.* 2nd ed. Cambridge: Cambridge University Press, 1978. Originally published in 1955 under the title, *Grimaldi, King of Clowns*, this is a biography of one of the first modern-era clowns.

Finley, Mitchel B. "Can We Laugh With the Church?" *Our Sunday Visitor Magazine*, Februry 5, 1984, pp. 8-9.

Finnigan, Dave. *The Joy of Juggling.* Available from the Juggle Bug, Inc. 23004 107th Place W, Edwards, Washington 98020. A basic manual on juggling.

Fiorenze, Francis. "Joy and Pain as Paradignatic for Language About God." in *Theology of Joy*, edited by Maetz and Jossua, New York: Herder and Herder, 1974, pp. 67-80. Discusses Kitamori's *Theology of the Pain of God.*

Fischer, Edward. "Humor is a Serious Matter." *Ave Maria*, October 29, 1955, p. 26. General Sketch of American humor.

*Fischer, Kathleen R. "Imagination: Becoming a Lost Sheep." *Modern Liturgy*, September 1984, pp. 14-15. On Spirituality mixing with imagination.

*_____. *The Inner Rainbow: The Imagination in Christian Life.* Paulist Press, 1983. On imagination and mystery, imagination and truth, imagination with others; and how artists help us pause, look, and see more clearly.

Fischer, Eugene J. "Divine Comedy: Humor in the Bible." *Religious Education*, November-December 1977, pp. 571-579.

Fitzpatrick, Mike, and Connolly, Tom. "Liturgy and Indian Powwow." *Modern Liturgy*, October 1976, p. 7. How a field mass moved into a pow wow.

_____. "Liturgy: in Time in Space." *Modern Liturgy*, October 1976, pp. 4-5. Roman Catholic liturgy and Native American communities.

_____. "A Reservation Wake." *Modern Liturgy*, September/October 1980, p. 40. A clown skit.

Fitzsimmons, Chris. "Body of Christ." *Modern Liturgy*, September/October 1980, p. 40. A clown skit.

Fleming, David C. *The Spiritual Exercises of St. Igantius: A Literal Translation and a Contemporary Reading*. St. Louis: Institute of Jesuit Sources, 1978.

Fleming, Peter J. "Liturgy and Life-Stories." *Modern Liturgy*, November/December 1976, pp. 4-5, 10-12.

*Folliet, Joseph. "Christian Humor." *Franciscan Herald*, June 1964, pp. 178-185, 191. A summary of Christian humorists through the centuries.

Fontana, John. "Be a Clown." *Ministries*, April 1980, p. 5. A brief introduction to clowning as a youth ministry.

Foote, Jennifer, "Belushi Lived Life in his Peculiar Way," *Oakland Tribune*, pp. A1, A2.

*Forbes, Patrick. "Gospel Fool." *1981 Clown, Mime, Puppet and Dance Workbeek*, 16 pages. Good, solid overview of the history of fools and clowns, and their powers to heal the Church. Also deals with liminality.

Fox, Matthew. Anything Fox writes provides lots of background and reflection on how scripture, tradition and mystical life support the useless ministry of the clown. See also his *Bear and Company* magazine, especially his issue on Ken Feit, Vol. 1, No. 5, 1981. Subscriptions are available from Bear and Co., Inc, 6 Vista Grande Court, Sante Fe, New Mexico 87501.

*_____. "A Eulogy Remembering Ken Feit and Other Cosmic Fools." *Bear and Company*, Vol. 1, No. 5, pp. 2-5. A great summary of Feit, both his life and work.

*_____. "Transcendence and More: About Ken Feit." *Bear and Company*, Vol. 1, No. 5, pp. 8-9. A collection of remembrances by various people who knew Ken.

Frank, Frederick. *Art as a Way: A Return to the Spritual Roots*. New York: Crossroad, 1981. Talks about art as transcendence, and art as a way of spirituality.

Freeling, Catherine. "Leonard Pitt: Mime." *The Berkeley Gazette*, pp. 22-24.

Freud, Sigmund. *On Creativity and the Unconscious.* Edited by Benjamin Nelson. New York: Harper and Row, 1958. Talks about the psychology of art, literature, love, and religion.

Friedman, Ann M. "Tips for Tellers of Tales." *Modern Liturgy,* November/December 1976, pp. 28-29.

Frosch, Thomas R. "Parody and the Contemporary Imagination." *Soundings,* Winter 1973, pp. 371-392.

Fry, Christopher. "Comedy," in *Comedy: Meaning and Form,* ed. by Robert W. Corrigen. Scranton: Chandler Pub. Co, 1965, pp. 15-17.

Fulco, William. "Jewish Storytelling and Anamnesis." *Modern Liturgy,* November/December 1976, pp. 8-9.

*Funk, Robert Walter. *Jesus as Precurser.* Philadelphia: Fortress Press, 1975.

_____. *Language, Hermeneutic, and Word of God: The Problem of Language in the New Testament and Contemporary Theology.* New York: Harper and Row, 1966.

*Gardner, Herb. *A Thousand Clowns.* New York: Random House, 1961. A great about someone who doesn't understand why life can't be more fun and spontaneous.

Garrett, Graeme. "My Brother Esau is a Hairy Man: an Encounter Between the Comedian and the Preacher." *Scottish Journal of Theology,* 1980, pp. 239-256.

Gates, Frieda. *North American Indian Masks: Craft and Legend.* New York: Walker and Co, 1982. Elementary introduction to various styles of masks, and how to make them. Simple versions.

Gay, Volney P. "Winnicott's Contribution to Religious Studies: the Resurrection of the Cultural Hero." *Journal of the American Academy of Religion,* September 1983, pp. 371-395.

Ghiselin, Brewster, ed. *The Creative Process.* New York: New American Library, 1952. Tells how different well known people have experienced the process.

Gibson, John H. "What Your Laughter Tells About You." *Catholic Digest,* September 1972, pp. 90-92. A brief overview of laughter and psychology.

Gilbert, E. Reid. "The Art of Silence." two pages.

Glass, Reneta. "The Clown." *The Candle,* a publication of the Christian Laymen of Chicago. Also in the *1980 Clown, Mime, Puppet and Dance Workbook,* 1 page. A good one-page description of clowning.

Glavich, Mary Kirene. "Let There Be Laughter." *Religion Teachers Journal*, September 1981, pp. 605-608. Describes Jewish humor as building on the three levels of family, society, and culture; describes growing up in a Brooklyn that seemed to foster Jewish comics.

Goldman, Albert. "Boy-man Schlemiel: Jewish Humor." *Commonweal*, September 29, 1967, pp. 605-608. Describes Jewish humor as building on the three levels of family society and culture; describes growing up in a Brooklyn that seemed to foster Jewish comics.

Goldstein, Jeffrey H. "The Healing Power of Laughter." *San Francisco Chronicle*, September 1, 1982, p. FF-1. Looks at the history of laughter in Western Society.

Good, Edwin. *Irony in the Old Testament.*

Grande, L.M. "Leaven of Laughter." *Today*, April 1960, pp. 33-35.

Grant, Lee. "Belushi Went For Hard Laughs, Hard Living." *Oakland Tribune*, pp. C1, C5.

Gray, Norma. "Ministrel Troubador Finds a Role Today." On "Pegasus" (Joe Rananda), and his entertaining children in the San Francisco Bay area.

Greeley, Andrew. "Humor and Ecclesiastical Ministry." in *Theology of Joy*, edited by Metz and Jossua, New York: Herder and Herder, 1974, pp. 134-140. On satire, and how laughter releases tension so that we can approach God directly.

Griffin, Robert. "Damn Everything but the Circus." *Our Sunday Visitor Magazine*, December 5, 1982, p. 14.

*Gritsch, Eric W. "Luther's Humor: Instrument of Witness." *Dialog*, Summer 1983, pp. 176-181. Good summary of Luther and his use of humor throughout his life and work.

Grock. *Life's a Lark*. Translated by Madge Pemberton. London: W. Heineman Ltd., 1931. Reprinted by Benjamin Blom, New York and London, 1969. Deals with his life as a clown.

Grottanelli, Cristiano. "Tricksters, Scape goats, Champions, Saviors." *History of Religions*, November 1983, pp. 117-139.

Groves, Jim, and Teigen, Terry. "Dramatizing Humor in Jonah, Chapter 4." *Modern Liturgy*, December/ January 1979, p. 8.

Guardini, Romano. "The Playfulness of the Liturgy." in *The Church and the Catholic and the Spirit of the Liturgy*. New York: Sheed and Ward, 1967, pp. 171-184.

Gunston, D. "A Gift from God." *Magnificat*, September 1962, pp. 25-28.

Haining, Peter. *The Legend of Charlie Chaplin.* London: W.H. Allen and Co, 1983. Nice collection of articles from people who knew Chaplin.

Hall, Edward T. *The Silent Language.* Garden City: Doubleday and Company.

*Ham, Susan J. "Who's Afraid of Santa Claus? Overcoming Fear of Costumed Characters: A Therapeutic Recreation Approach." *Program Trends in Therapeutic Recreation.* 3 pages. Insights of how to overcome children's fear of people in costumes.

Hamblin, Kay. *Mime: A Playbook of Silent Fantasy.* Garden City: Doubleday and Company, 1978.

Hamilton Edith. "Aristophanes and the Old Comedy." in *The Greek Way to Western Civilization*, Mentor.

Hamilton, Kenneth, and Haverluck, Robert Thomas. "Laughter and Vision." *Soundings*, Summer 1972, pp. 163-177. Good overview of comedy, celebration, and laughter in the Church.

Hammarstrom, David Lewis. *Behind the Big Top/* Cranbury, NJ: A.S. Barnes and Co. 1980. A behind-the-scenes account.

Hammer-Higgins, Paula. "The Gospel Clown." A handbook for "Clowns of the Covenant," Lexington, KY. 12 pages. A nice gathering of materials for clown groups.

*Harper, Valene. "Priest's Little Big Show Blends Circus, Religion." *National Catholic Reporter*, November 23, 1973, pp. 1,15. Good presentation of Weber's quarter-ring circus ministry.

Harris, Maria. "Religious Educators and the Comic Vision." *Religious Education*, July-August 1980, pp. 422-432.

Hart, Ray. *Unfinished Man and the Imagination.* New York: Seabury Press, 1979. Deals with theology as herneneutic, imagination, revelation, and creativity.

Hartisch, Karl "Whitey." *Introduction to Clowning.* Reprinted by Clowns of America, Inc. Covers all aspects of clowning including the business side.

Harzberg, Hiler, and Moss, Arthur. *Slapstick and Dumbell: A Casual Survey of Clowns and Clowning.* New York: Joseph Lawren, 1924. Personal impressions about the history and importance of the resurgence of clowning in the secular arena in the 1920s.

Hawes, Bill. *The Puppet Book.* San Francisco: Beta Books, 1977.

Hayne, Donald. "Ingredient Sadly Lacking: Humor." *Commonweal*, May 6, 1938, pp. 42-43. He says Catholics take themselves too seriously: echos what many other Catholic writers say.

Hays, E. "Feast of Fools." *Sign*, April 1980, pp. 20-21.

*Hebblethwaithe, Peter. "Clowns for Christ." *Tablet* (London), September 18, 1982, pp. 931-2. Presents a good argument for the ministry of jesting within the Church.

———————. "Joking Apart." *Tablet*, January 29, 1972, p. 79. On the nature of the Catholic joke; says Catholic wit came about to offset Puritanism.

> *His Offering.*
> He offered the people a gospel of
> laughter, popcorn and balloons. But
> they thought him a performer left
> over from last year's circus.
>
> No one understood his gift: a flower
> pulled from behind his ear that was
> started from the water of a tear.
> No one knew his final goodbye
> promised an unexpected hello.
>
> Mark Wiley

from *alive now!* March/April 1979, by The Upper Room. Used by permission of the author.

Heifetz, Harold, ed. *Zen and Hasidism*. Thesophical Publishing House, 1978. Compares the two spiritual disciplines, especially the essence of joyfulness in both.

*Henkelmann, David and Mel. Coversations, 1981-1982. Insights from these two wonderful, creative clowns, puppeteers, and dramatists in the Moravian Church.

* ———————. "Worship in White Face." 3 pages. A good example of a worship service done by clowns in complete silence; with stage directions.

Henry, R.T. "Mimicry in Preaching," *Homiletic and Pastoral Review*, August 1931, pp. 1142-1147.

"Here Come the Clowns." *Catholic Digest*, May 1961, pp. 40-42. Reprint of "Bring on the Clowns," *Aramco World Magazine*, October 1960. A quick look at the history of clowns.

Herrigel, Eugen. *Zen in the Art-of Archery*. New York: Pantheon, 1953. Speaks of the unity of life in what we do, think, breathe.

Heschel, Abraham J. *The Prophets: An Introduction*. New York: Harper and Row, 1962. A good introduction to the prophets.

Hess, M. Whitcomb. "The Comic Spirit." *Catholic World*, January 1954, pp. 273-277. General treatment of the use of humor and laughter.

Hiltner, Seward. "The Minister in the Human Circus." *Patoral Psychology*, December 1971, pp. 13-20. How the pastor can be more effective by being a clown. Related to the article by Heije Faber.

*Hineline, Barbara. Unpublished parable on why women aren't in Seminary. January 1981, Berkeley, California. A modern parable that confuses the intellect, but still gets its point across.

Hobbs, Edward. "A Theology of Visual Art." Lecture delivered at the Graduate Theological Union, Berkeley, California on December 18, 1981.

Hogan, Mary Ann. "Taking Humor Seriously: Laughter Gets a Place in the Medicine Cabinet." *Eastbay Today*, Oakland, California, April 26, 1982, pp. C1, C5.

Holbert, John C. "Deliverance Belongs to Yahweh: Satire in the Book of Jonah." *Journal for the Study of the Old Testament*, 1981, pp. 29-81.

Holmer, Paul L. "Something About What Makes It Funny." *Soundings*, Summer 1974, pp. 157-174.

Holmes, Urban T. "Liminality and Liturgy." *Worship*, Vol. 47, No. 7, pp. 386-397.

_____. *Ministry and Imagination*. New York: Seabury Press, 1976. This work sets the theological stage for doing any kind of imaginative work. Careful Scholarship.

"Holy Laughter." *Parabola*, February 1979, pp. 48-53. Quotes from various writers on the subject of laughter.

Hommes, Tjaard. "Authentic Ministry." *Lutheran Quarterly*, February 1977, pp. 58-65. On ministers, clowns, and masks; putting them on and taking them off.

Huddleston, D. "Clowns are Here to Stay!" *Family Digest*, August 1970, pp. 2-11.

Hugill, Beryl. *Bring on theClowns*. Seacaucus, NJ: Chartwell Books, Inc., 1980. A nice pictoral history of clowns.

Huizinga, Johan. *Homo Ludens: A Study of the Play Element in Culture*. Boston: Beacon Press, 1950. A seminal work on the importance of play in life.

Humorneutics. A monthly humor service for sermons, lessons, dinners, etc. PO Box 911, Dept. ML, Burbank, CA 91503. 1 year for $25.

Hunt, Douglas and Kari. *Pantomine: The Silent Theatre.* New York: Atheneum, 1966.

Hunt, Wilfred. "Random Comments on Mime, Art and Life." 1979 *Clown, Mime, Puppet and Dance Workbook*, 4 pages.

Hunter, Nadene D. "Observations of Clowning with and for Handicapped Persons," *1982 Clown, Mime, Puppet and Dance Workbeek*, 2 pages.

Hurwitt, Robert. "According to Hoyle." *East Bay Express,* Oakland, CA, August 2, 1983, p. 10. (Geoff Hoyle)

Hvidberg, Fleming. *Weeping and Laughter in the Old Testament.*

*Hyers, Conrad. "Christian Humor: Uses and Abuses of Laughter." *Dialog*, Summer 1983, pp. 198-203. Portions excerpted from his book *Comic Vision*; speaks of how faith is a balance between pride and unbelief.

*_____. "Comedy and Creation." *Theology Today,* April 1982, pp. 17-26. Portions excerpted from his biik, *Comic Vision*; speaks of comedy as an affirmation of creatureliness, rather than an escape from.

_____. "Comic Profanation of the Sacred," in *Holy Laughter*, edited by Hyers. New York: Seabury Press, 1969, pp. 10-27. Speaks of how there is a lack of systematic treatment of humor and holiness; and how humor is a needed part of much of life.

*_____. *The Comic Vision and the Christian Faith: A Celebration of Life and Laughter.* New York: Pilgrim Press, 1981. A great book spanning the subjects of clowns, fools, and jesters throughout history, secular and sacred; and written in an essay style.

_____. "The Comic Vision in a Tragic World." *Christian Century*, April 20, 1983, pp. 363-367. Portions excerpted from his book *Comic Vision*; deals with comic virtues as compared to biblical virtues.

_____. "The Dialectic of the Sacred and the Comic." *Cross Currents*, Winter 1969, pp. 69-79. Appears in related form in *Holy Laughter*, ed. by Hyers, New York: Seabury Press, 1969, pp. 208-240.

_____. "A Funny Faith." One World, July-August 1982, pp. 10-11. Humor as ecumenical entertainment.

*_____. ed. *Holy Laughter: Essays on Religion in the Comic Perspective.* New York: Seabury Press, 1969. Articles by such people as Lynch, Scott, Zucker, Miller, Niebuhr, and Trueblood. Unfortunately this book is now out of print.

_____. "Introduction" to *Holy Laughter*, ed. by Hyers; New York: Seabury Press, 1969, pp. 1-7. Speaks of the comic dimension in religion, and introduces the articles in the book.

*_____. "The Nativity as Divine Comedy." *The Christian Century*, December 11, 1974, pp. 1168-1172. Deals with the biblical themes of putting down the proud, and elevating the humble; and shows how clowns do this.

*_____. "The Recovery of Simplicity." *The Christian Century*, August 7, 1974, pp. 768-771. Clowns mediate between the sacred and the profane, those in-between times when life just is. The simplicity of children is held up as a third way of living.

*_____. *Zen and the Comic Spirit.* London: Rider and Co., 1973; and Philadelphia; Westminster Press, 1974. This book makes some important contributions to the Christian understanding of religion and humor. This book is also out of print.

Ice, Jackson Lee. "Notes Towards a Theology of Humor." *Religion in Life*, Autumn 1973, pp. 388-400.

In Unity. "Clown Ministry." Februry/March 1980, p. 5.

Istas, Joan L. "Brightening Life with Laughter." *Columbia*, February 1982, pp. 18-23.

Jaggi, Willy. *Harlekin.* Basel: Basilus Presse, 1959. Although this book is in German, there are many pictures of clowns from the stage, the circus, and from art around the world. Such pictures are hard to find, especially in one book.

*Jeffrey, Graham. His works are published in England, and some of them are out of print. But they are worth the search: *Barnabas* (1976); *Barnabas Again* (1976); *The Barnabas Bible; Bush Brother;* and *Thank You For Coming: Gospel Reflections* (1982). Published by Mowbray, Oxford, England. Jeffrey has a nice way of seeing the Bible through fresh eyes, via the bumbling disciple Barnabas and the cartoon strip format.

Jenkins, Ron. "Two Way Mirrors." *Parabola*, summer 1981, pp. 17-21. On Bali masks.

Jeremias, Joachim. *The Parables of Jesus.* Translated by S.H. Hooke, London: SCM Press, 1963, rev. ed. Good study on the handling of the parables by the early Church.

Jewett, Paul K. "Wit and Humor of Life." *Christianity Today*, June 8, 1959, pp. 7-9. Christianity as the religion of Joy.

Jilek, Wilfgang G. *Indian Healing: Shamanic Ceremonialism in the Pacific Northwest Today.* Blaine, WA: Hancock House Publishers, Ltd, 1982. Covers the psychology of shamanic healing.

John, P.M. "Joke and the Punchline: On interpreting Myths in Indian Culture." *Religion and Society*, December 1975, pp. 63-76.

Johnston, Robert. *The Christian at Play*. Frand Rapids: Eerdmans, 1983. Deals with the theology of play.

Johnstone, Keith. *Impro: Improvisation and the Theatre*. New York: Theatre Arts Book, 1980. Good treatment of the subject, with techniques and exercises.

Jones, Peter W. "Christian Laughter." *New Blackfriars*, Summer 1973, pp. 421-427. An overview with the touch of the theology of play.

Johnson, Jakob. *Humor and Irony in the New Testament*.

Jordan, Clarence. *The Cotton Patch Version of Luke and Acts*. Chicago: Association Press, 1969. His colloquial translations of the New Testament provide a first step for seeing the scriptures as a new comer. See his other versions on the rest of the New Testament.

Kaasa, Harris. "Confessions of a Serious-Minded Joker." *Dialog*, Summer 1983, pp. 171-175. Personal reflections about how humor and seriousness are both needed to deal with the paradox of faith.

Kadinsky, Wassily. *On the Spiritual in Art*, 1914.

*Kadowaki, J.K. *Zen and the Bible: A Priest's Experience*. London: Routledge and Kegan Paul, 1980. Compares Ignatian exercises and Zen Koans as ways of entering into stories and making them one's own. See especially Chapter 17, on "The super-logic of the 'fool.'"
""

Kaiser, Walter. *Praisers of Folly*. Cambridge: Harvard University Press, 1963.

*Kazantzakis, Nikos. *Zorba the Greek*. trans. Carl Wedman, New York: Simon and Schuster, 1952. A great story of a clown in person's clothing. An inspirational classic on living with zest!

*Keen, Sam. *Apology for Wonder*. New York: Harper and Row, 1969.

*_____. *To a Dancing God*. New York: Harper and Row, 1970. A great book of reflections on the humanity of God.

Kehl, Tim. "Be a Clown." *Modern Liturgy*, August 1981, p. 32. Make-up hints.

*_____. "Clown Message: Christian Message." *Modern Liturgy*, August 1981, pp. 4-5. This is a short version of his full presentation on the theology of clowning found in the 1978 *Shoddy Pad*, but it is easier to get to.

*_____. "Getting Started in Clown Ministry." *Shoddy*

Pad, 1978, by the Clown Ministry Cooperative. Paired with his "Theology of Clowning" article.

*_____. "The Theology of Clowning." *Shoddy Pad*, 1978, by the United Methodist Communications, Nashville, Tennessee, 6 pages. Kehl shows how the clown can be compared with Christ as a symbol of hope, joy, and as fulfilling the roles of non-conformist, vulnerable lover, and servant figure. Also has ideas for clown services, and hints for clown make-up. Excellent presentation. Also includes a resource list.

Keillor, Garrison. *Happy to be Here: Even More Stories and Comic Pieces*. New York: Atheneum Publishers, 1981; Penguin, 1983. A nice collection of witty stories from the creator of Public Radio's "Prairie Home Companion."

_____. *News From Lake Wobegon*, four cassettes produced by Minnesota Public Radio, 1983. Stories from the "Prairie Home Companion" show, each tape focuses on a different season.

Kelly, Emmett. With F. Beverly Kelley. *Clown*. New York: Prentice-Hall, 1954. His autobiography upto 1954: development of Weary Willie.

_____. "The Day the Clowns Cried." *Catholic Digest*, from *Clown*, by Emmett Kelley.

Kennedy, Jeremiah. "The Glory of Laughter." Photo-essay in *Sign*, September 1972, pp. 10-16. Nice presentation, with nice quotes and pictures.

Kenny, Herbert A. "Gaiety of Catholicism: Lack of Wit in Catholic Magazines." *Catholic World*, August 1949, pp. 341-343. A plea for good Catholic adult humor in Catholic magazines.

Kerr, Hugh T. "Editorial: Not Like They Used To." *Theology Today*, April 1975, pp. 1-9.

*Kerr, Walter. *The Silent Clowns*. New York: Knopf, 1975. The definitive book on Chaplin, Keaton, Lloyd, etc.

_____. *Tragedy and Comedy*. New York: Simon and Schuster, 1967.

Kierkegaard, Soren. *The Concept of Irony* translated by Lee Capel. Bloomington, Indiana University Press, 1965.

Kiffmeyer, John. "Translating Scripture to Hear Humor." *Modern Liturgy*, December/January 1979, pp. 6-7.

Killinger, Jack, ed. *The 11 O'Clock News*. Nashville: Abingdon Press, 1975, esp. pp. 25-30.

King, J.C.H. *Portrait Masks From the North West Coast of*

America. London: Thames and Hudson, 1979. Introduces and compares the masks of five North West Coast Indian tribes.

Kipnis, Claude. *The Mime Book.* A basic how to instructional guide.

Klien, Allen. *The Whole Mirth Catalogue*, San Francisco.

Kloos, Bob. "In Illo Tempore." *Modern Liturgy*, March 1983, pp. 4-5. Looks at the comparison between the avangelist and the storyteller.

Knox, Israel. "The Traditional Roots of Jewish Humor." in *Holy Laughter*, ed. by Conrad Hyers. New York: Seabury Press, 1969, pp. 150-165. On the nature of Jewish humor; from *Judaism*, Summer 1963, pp. 327-337.

Kopp, Sheldon, B. *If You Meet the Buddha on the Road, Kill Him.* New York: Bantam Books, 1976. On finding out who you are, and being accepting and affirming of what you find.

Kuntz, Bob. "Christian Side of Clowning." *1979 Clown, Mime, Puppet and Dance Workbook*, 5 pages. Notes on clowning for Church groups, with a long list of Bible passages useful in clowning.

Landmann, Michael. "Melancholies on Fulfilment." in *Theology of Joy*, edited by Metz and Jossua, New York: Herder and Herder, 1974, pp. 31-45. On how the victories of this world always fade, and their is a need for victories of another sort.

*Lane, Belden C. "The Spirituality and Politics of Holy Folly." *Christian Century*, December 15, 1982, pp. 1281-1286. How folly can save us from believing that reality is the last word on anything.

Lang, Andrew. He has put together a 14 volume collection of fairy tales from around the world. Available in paperback from Dover Books, many of them are entitled with colors, such as *The Green Fairy Tale Book.* Good resources for storytellers.

*Larsen, Stephen, and Larsen, Robin. "The Healing Mask." *Parabola*, Summer 1981, pp. 78-84. On ones own mask, and the healing masks from several cultures.

*_____. *The Shaman's Doorway.* New York: Harper and Row, 1977. Good introduction to the connections between Black Elk and Jung, Yoga and comic books, belief and orthodoxy, the arts of the shaman and the arts of the clown; a cross cultural study.

Laux, P. "The Gift of Laughter." *Catholic School Journal*, December 1969, p. 25.

Lax, Eric. *On Being Funny: Woody Allen and Comedy.* New York: Charterhouse, 1975.

Leeming, David. "The Hodja." *Parabola*, February 1979, pp. 84-89. About a major fool in the Islamic tradition.

Levenson, Jon D. The Poronomasia of Solomon's Seventh Petition." *Hebrew Annual Review*, 1982, pp. 135-138.

Levi-Strauss, Claude. *The Way of Masks*, trns. by Sylvia Modelski. Vancouver/Toronto: Douglas-McIntyre Co., 1982. On the interaction of art and myth, focused on North West Coast Indians.

Levy, Robert J. "Apologia Pro Von Hunga." *Dialog*, Summer 1983, pp. 182-186. Humorous story about theologians and eating.

Liebenow, Kurt Steven. *Being Shaved by Laughter*, Lake Mills, WI: Lambda Mu Publications, 1971. About how beards can be masks, moustaches can be half-masks, and how laughter is closer to fact than reality.

Litherland, Janet. *The Clown as Minister*. Contemporary Drama Service: Downers Grove, IL. Skits and ideas.

_____. *The Clown as Minister II*. Contemporary Drama Service. More skits and ideas.

_____. *The CLown Ministry Handbook*. Downers Grove, IL: Contemporary Drama Service, 1982. Elementary introduction to clowning in church. Briefly covers the basic areas.

Loeschke, Maravene. *All About Mime: Understanding and Performing the Expressive Silence*. Englewood Cliffs: Prentice-Hall, 1982.

Long, Louis V. "Ideas: New Ideas, Old Ideas, Funny Ideas." *1982 Clown, Mime, Puppet and Dance Work-Book*, 11 pages. 200 ideas for getting a start in clowning.

*"Love, Laughter, and Healing: True Tales from the Medical Profession." *New Age*, April 1983, pp. 32-41. Adapted from the proceeding of "The Role of Love and Laughter in the Healing Process" conference held by the interface foundation in November 1982. An important summary of the benefit of therapeutic clowning.

Lynch, William. *Christ and Apollo: Dimensions of the Literary Imagination*. New York: Sheed and Ward, 1969.

_____. *Faith and Imagination*. New York: Paulist Press, 1979.

_____. "The Humanity of Comedy." in *Holy Laughter*, ed. by Conrad Hyers. New York: Seabury Press, 1969, pp. 28-44. Deals with literature; from *Christ and Apollo: The Dimension of the Literary Imagination*. New York: Sheed and Ward, 1960.

_____. *Images of Hope: Imagination as Healer of the Hopeless*. Helicon Press, 1965.

*_____. "The Life of Faith and Imagination." *The Month*, January 1979, pp. 5-9. Marks out three parallels between theology and art — common problems, their ontological natures, and the presence of imagination as a vehicle for bearing truths.

_____. "Theology and the Imagination III: The Problem of Comedy." *Thought*, pp. 18-36. Talks about the differences between art and comedy.

MacNair, A. Stanley. *There's a Rhino in My Soup: Or How I Learned to Digest Things With Points.* Los Angeles: Animal Crackers Press, 1980. True confessions of a pastor who never thought Church wasn't a funny place to be religious. Good stuff.

Makarius, L. "Ritual Clowns and Symbolic Behavior." tr. by R. Makarius. *Diogenes*, Spring 1970, pp. 44-73.

Malin, Edward. *A World of Faces: Masks of the North West Coast Indians.* Portland: Timber Press, 1978. The role of masks in the life of the people.

Mann, Beverly. "Marcel Marceau." *San Francisco Chronicle*, February 7, 1982, Datebook Section.

Manning-Sanders, Ruth. *The English Circus.* London: Werner Laurie, 1952. Chapter 21 is on clowns and Augustes.

Manousos, D. "That Deadpan Catholic Press." *Today*, November 1959, pp. 32-33.

Marceau, Marcel. "The Adventure of Silence." in *Mimes on Miming*, ed. by Bari Rolfe, pp. 146-149.

_____. "The Art of Mime." *Quest*, September 1981, pp. 39-43.

_____. "The Art of Silence: Pantomimes with Marcel Marceau." films, *Encyclopedia Brittanica Films*, 425 N. Michigan Avenue, Chicago, IL. 13 films, in color, ranging from 7 to 17 minutes in length.

_____. "Language of the Heart." *Theatre Arts 42*, March 1958, pp. 58-59. On why he became a mime.

_____. "Silence Broken." *Los Angeles Times*, August 18, 1968, pp. 1, 30, 40 (Calendar Section).

_____. *The Story of Bip.* New York: Harper and Row, 1976.

_____. Article by Beverly Mann, *San Francisco Chronicle*, "Marcel Marceau," February 7, 1982. Datebook Section.

_____. Book by Martin, Ben. *Marcel Marceau:*

Master of Mime. New York: Paddington Press, Grosset and Dunlap, 1978.

——————. Book by Mendoza, George. *The Marcel Marceau Alphabet Book.* Garden City: Doubleday and Company, 1970.

——————. Interviews by Verriest-Lefert. *Marcel Marceau ou L'aventure du Silence.* Paris: Descleau de Broumer, 1974. Translated by Bari Rolfe, and revised by Marceau.

Mardon, M. "Ring Around the Loon." *Tablet,* December 19, 1959, pp. 1111.

Martin, Ben. *Marcel Marceau: Master of Mime.* New York: Paddington Press, Grosset and Dunlap, 1978. A visual Biography: nicely done.

Masse, Benjamin, L. "With Cap and Bells." *Catholic World,* May 1935, pp. 177-183. Good; on the surge of Catholic satirists in the 1930s.

Mast, Gerald. *The Comic Mind: Comedy and the Movies.* Chicago: University of Chicago Press, 1979.

Mather, Judson. "The Comic Art of the Book of Jonah." *Soundings,* Fall 1982, pp. 280-291. Comic characterizations in religious biography.

Mattingly, Terry. "Doug Marlette: Tragedy and Bitter Laughter." *Christian Century,* June 20-27, 1984, pp. 631-632. On Marlette's "Kudzu" comic strip; Marlette feels that everything is religious, because everything involves somebody's God.

Maurer, Irene. *The Art of the Mime.* Boston: Expression Company, 1960. On the history and principles of mime.

Maxwell, Farley. "Biblical Point: Counter Point — Dramatizing the Dilemma of Preaching." *Modern Liturgy,* December/January 1979, p. 7. On Jesus and the meaning of his parables.

May, Rollo. *The Courage to Create.* New York: Norton and Co., 1975. Creativity from a psychological point of view.

Mazer, Eileen. "Healing Laughter." *Catholic Digest,* August 1981, pp. 6, 8, 10, 12. From *Prevention;* deals with an overview of laughter and therapeutic benefits.

McBride, M. "Give Us This Day Our Daily Wit." *St. Anthony Messenger,* July 1973, pp. 10-14.

McBride, Stewart. "Christian Clowns Preach the Word — Silently." *Christian Science Monitor,* September 10, 1981, pp. B11-13. A report of the 1981 Clown, Mime, Puppet and Dance Workshop in Berkeley, California.

McClendon, James Wm, Jr. *Biography as Theology: How Life Stories Can Remake Todays Theology.* Nashville: Abingdon Press, 1974. Looks at how the lives of people can be a resource for doing theology.

McCord, James I. "On Getting and Keeping a Sense of Humor: Farewell Remarks to Graduating Class 1973." *Princeton Seminary Bulletin,* Winter 1975, pp. 48-51.

*McFague, Sallie. *Speaking in Parables: A Study in Metaphor and Theology.* Philadelphia: Fortress Press, 1975. Looks at how poems, stories and autobiographies can be resources for doing theology. Also discusses parabolic theology, or "intermediary theology" that lives between the lives of people and systematic theology.

*McGinley, Phyllis. "The Wit of Saints." *Catholic Digest,* August 1962, pp. 12-18. Condensed from *Vogue Magazine*; deals with how canonization demands proof of joy in the candidate.

McHugh, L.C. "Should There Be Humor in the Catholic Press?" *America,* May 9, 1959, pp. 301-301. Editorial on the rarity of real humor in the Catholic press; humor as a part of the interpretation of life.

McKenna, Megan. "Mime and Ministry." *Modern Liturgy,* September/October 1980, pp. 4-5. An overview.

*McLelland, Joseph C. *The Clown and the Crocodile.* Richmond: John Knox Press, 1970. Starts with the hypothesis that the only appropriate response to God's essentially useless creation is neither tragedy nor rationalism but laughter; and the book takes off from there.

_____. "Doxology as Suspension of the Tragic." *Theology Today,* July 1974, pp. 114-120.

McVicar, Wes. *Clown Act Omnibus.* New York: Association Press, 1960. Over two-hundred clown skits.

Melendez, Theresa. "Coyote: Towards a Definition of a Concept." *Aztlan* 13, Spring-Fall 1982, pp. 295-307.

Meltz, Ken. "The Word, Music, and Imagination." *Modern Liturgy,* April 1983, pp. 8-10. Ritual in the Liturgy of the Word.

Menzoda, George. *The Marcel Marceau Alphabet Book.* Garden City: Doubleday and Company, 1970.

Meredith, George. "An Essay on Comedy." in *Comedy,* edited by Wylie Sypher. Garden City: Doubleday and Company, 1956. Includes an essay by Bergson on laughter.

Merton, Thomas. *Seasons of Celebration*. New York: Farrar, Straus and Giroux, 1965. In the chapter on Easter, Merton speaks on folly for Christ — yurodivetsvo; in the chapter on the Good Samaritan, he speaks of chesed, and the chasid who is made comical by mercy.

_____. "Theology of Creativity." *American Benedictine Review*, September-December 1960, pp. 197-213.

_____. *The Wisdom of the Desert: Sayings from the Desert Fathers of the Fourth Century*. New York: New Directions, 1960.

Messer, Ron. "A Jungian Interpretation of the Relationship of Culture: Hero and Trickster Figure Within Chippewa Mythology." *Studies in Religion*, Summer 1982, pp. 309-320. Includes a discussion of Longfellow's Hiawatha.

_____. "Nanabozho: History and Mythology." *Bulletin of Bibliography*, December 1983, pp. 242-251.

Metz, Johann Baptist. "Editorial: Joy and Grief, Cheerfulness, Melancholy and Humor or 'The Difficulty of Saying Yes.'" in *Theology of Joy*, edited by Metz and Jossua, New York: Herder and Herder, 1974, pp. 7-12. On the tasks of fundamental theology; introduction to the book; and on the dynamics of Christian joy.

*_____, and Jossua, Jean-Pierre, editors. *Theology of Joy*. New York: Herder and Herder, 1974. Articles by David Steere, Michael Landmann, Eugen Biser, Francis Fiorenze, Gerard Bessiere, Jacques Colette, Ernesto Cardenal, Dorothee Solle, Fulbert Steffensky, Norbert Schiffers, Andrew Greeley, Mac Tannenbaum, Heinrich Boll.

Meyer, Charles. *How to be a Clown*. McKary, 1977.

Miffleton, Jack. "How to Entertain a Dinosaur (Without disturbing you mother)." *Modern Liturgy*, January 1977, p. 28. On the use of fantasy meditation.

Miller, Barbara Stoler. "Moving Designs of Masked Emotion." *Parabola*, Summer 1981, pp. 85-89. Uses of masks in Southern Indian Dance Dramas.

Miller, David L. *Gods and Games: Towards a Theology of Play*. New York: Harper and Row, 1974.

Miller, Donald F. "A Time for Laughter, A Time for Dancing." *Liguorian*, June 1971, pp. 9-13. How a sense of humor can help you cope with life's inconsistencies.

Miller, Henry. *The Smile at the Foot of the Ladder*. New Directions.

Miller, Samuel H. "The Clown in Contemporary Art." *Theology*

Today, October 1967, pp. 318-328. Also in *Holy Laughter*, edited by Conrad Hyers. New York: Seabury Press, 1969, pp. 89-102. Basically works off the use of metaphors; and the concepts that humor is human, and meaning is transcendent. He feels there is so little room for the clown because there is so little room for Christ; theology of culture perspective.

Mills, Bart. "Time Hopping with a Python." *San Francisco Chronicle*, November 1, 1981, pp. 25-26, Datebook Section. About the movie "Time Bandits," and looking at fairy tales in a new way.

Modern Liturgy Magazine. Comes out eight times a year, with ideas on how to improve/change/creatively innovate your worship environment. Each issue deals with one theme. "Humor in Liturgy" was the theme of the December/January 1979 issue (6:8); "Liturgical Mime" in the September/October 1980 issue (7:6); and "Clowning in Liturgy" in the August 1981 issue (8:5). Subscriptions available from Resource Publications, 160 E. Virginia St. Suite 290, San Jose, CA 95112, or phone (408) 286-8505. Most back issues can be purchased.

Moody, Raymond. *Laugh after Laugh: The Healing Power of Humor*. Headwaters Press, 1978.

Moon, Clarice. *Here Come the Clowns*. Downers Grove: Contemporary Drama Service. Twenty short skits.

*Morris, Colin. *The Hammer of the Lord*. Nashville: Abingdon Press, 1973. Pages 88-100 on the clown as a symbol of hope are especially good; Jesus as clown; Chaplin; Humor.

Morrison, Timothy. "Easter Sunrise Service." *1979 Clown, Mime, Puppet and dance Workbook*, 5 pages.

*Mossman, James Frank. "The Clown." *Clown, Mime, Puppet and Dance Workbook*, 2 pages. The inner feelings of the person as the whiteface is put on; the dying to oneself and the rebirth.

Motter, Eileen. "Applying Clown Make-up and Developing Your Own Clown Character." *1982 Clown, Mime, Puppet and Dance Workbook*, 15 pages.

_____. "Clown Graffitti." *1982 Clown, Mime, Puppet and Dance Workbook*, 1 page.

_____. "Clown Ministry Guidelines." *1982 Clown, Mime, Puppet and Dance Workbook*, 1 page.

Moynahan, Michael. "Clowns and Sacraments." *Modern Liturgy*, August 1981, pp. 8-9. Makes connections between the two.

*_____. "Discovering God's Gift of Humor Through Liturgical Mime." *Modern Liturgy*, June/July 1979, pp. 6-7. Drama is an effective way to articulate sacramental experiences for children; a five-step approach.

_____. "Discovering the Experience of Sacrament Through Mime." *Modern Liturgy*, 7:4, pp. 6-7.

*_____. "Drama Brings God's Word into the Present." *Modern Liturgy*, February 1983, pp. 28-29. How to create a liturgical drama.

_____. "The Family That Plays Together Prays Together." *Modern Liturgy*, 5:4, pp. 5, 14.

_____. *How The Word Became Flesh*. San Jose: Resource Publications, 1981. Good source of story dramas for worship and religious education by an educator and a performer.

_____. "Improvisational Exercises." *1980 Clown, Mime, Puppet and Dance Workbook*, 5 pages.

_____. "Mime: Allowing the Word to Become Flesh." 8 pages. A version of "The Word Becomes Flesh," *Group Magazine*.

_____. "Mime: Characterization (Parts 1 and 2)." Class Handout.

_____. "Mime Exercises." *1980 Clown, Mime, Puppet and Dance Workbook*, 6 pages.

_____. "Mime for the Beginner." *Modern Liturgy*, September/October 1979, pp. 8, 39. All people pantomime. Three exercises to bring this out.

*_____. "Mime and Worship." *1981 Clown, Mime, Puppet and Dance Workbook*, 8 pages. Also in *Shoddy Pad*, 1981 series, published by United Methodist Communications, Nashville, Tennesse. Good for the theory behind mime, with guidelines for dramatizing in worship.

_____. "Miracle Stories Come Alive!! Through Drama." *Modern Liturgy*, May 1984, pp. 2, 15-16.

_____. *Once Upon a Parable: Dramas for Worship and Religious Education*. Ramsey, NJ: Paulist Press, 1984. Story dramatizations with full details about presenting them.

*_____. "Proclamation." *Modern Liturgy*, December/January 1979, pp. 8-9. Ways of proclaiming and presenting scripture.

*_____. "Puppets and Worship." *Modern Liturgy*, August 1982, pp. 4-5, 16-17. A good preparation of using puppets in worship.

*_____. "The Word Becomes Flesh: The Art of Mime." *Group*, June-August 1980, pp. 16-19. Talks about Marceau, the four types of mime, how the Berkeley Liturgical Drama Guild works, with guidelines, resources, and the Buried Treasure script.

Mudd, C.P. "Arts Come Home." *Modern Liturgy*, 8:5, pp. 20, 29. On using arts in worship, creatively.

Mueller, W.R. "God's Fools: Biblical and Modern." (reprint) *Theology Today*, January 1967, pp. 538-550.

Mullen, Wilbur. "Toward a Theology of Humor." (with a response by Ray S. Anderson) *Christian Scholars' Review*, 1973, pp. 3-14.

Mura, Dave. "Clown, Mime, Puppet and Dance Ministry and the Church." *1982 Clown, Mime, Puppet and Dance Workbook*. Why clowns are in Church.

_____. "Epiphany Mime." *Modern Liturgy*, Auguat 1981, pp. 38-39. A description and a script to work with.

Murray, Edward. "The Dionysian Ego of Norman O. Brown." MA Thesis, Pacific School of Religion, 1976. Includes a Dionysian Theology — a theology of dance.

Myers, Rawley. "Joy to the World." *Homilectic and Pastoral Review*, October 1980, pp. 20-24. How humor is a part of life; focuses on Pope John 23, and Bishop Sheen, etc.

National Catholic Reporter, August 28, 1981. "Compassionate Clown Dead in Auto Crash." On the death of Ken Feit, Itinerant Fool. Message by Matthew Fox provides an overview to Feit's life and work.

*Navone, John and Cooper, Thomas. *Tellers of the Word*. New York: LeJacq Pub, 1981. Excellent study of the theology of story.

Neal, Robert E. *In Praise of Play*. New York: Harper and Row, 1978; with bibliography.

*Neihardt, John. *Black Elk Speaks*. University of Nebraska Press, 1979. A solid presentation on the place of Heyhokas in the Sioux tribe, and on the life of Black Elk.

Niccolls, Tom. "Clowning for the Lord." *Commique*, March 1979, magazine of the Synod of the Covenant, the United Presbyterian Church in the United States of America. Also in the *1979 Clown, Mime, Puppet and Dance Workbook*. Tells how Niccolls was led to become a clown, and what clowning means to him.

_____. "Clowning in Worship." *Shoddy Pad*, Clown Ministry Cooperative.

_____. "The Comic Vision and the Stories of David." *Encounter*, Simmer 1981, pp. 277-283. Deals with the comic touches throughout the stories.

_____. "Flea Circus." *1980 Clown, Mime, Puppet and Dance Workbook*, 4 pages. On how to put on a flea circus.

_____. "God's Amazing Love: A Youth Rally Vircus Program." 8 pages.

_____. "Holy Laughter." *1979 Clown, Mime, Puppet and Dance Workbook*, 1 page.

_____. "The Praise of Folly." *Calliope*, columns from 1978-1981. Also in the *1980* and *1981 Clown, Mime, Puppet and Dance Workbooks*. On a variety of topics, short discussions.

_____. "Tomfoolery." *1979 Clown, Mime, Puppet and Dance Workbook*, 1 page. Why he clowns as part of his chaplaincy at Hiram College.

_____. "Upside Down Service." *1980 Clown, Mime, Puppet and Dance Workbook*, 4 pages A meditation and worship service program.

Nichols, Sallie. "The Wisdom of the Fool," (Tarot) *Psychological Perspectives*, Spring 1983, pp. 97-116.

Nicoll, Allardyce. *Masks, Mimes and Miracles*. New York: Cooper Square Publication, 1931, 1963.

_____. *The World of Harlequin:A Critical Study*. Cambridge: Cambridge University Press, 1963. On the Commedia dell' Arte.

Niebuhr, Reinhold. "Humor and Faith." in *Holy Laughter*, ed. by Conrad Hyers. New York: Seabury Press, 1969, pp. 134-149. From a social ethics viewpoint; from *Discerning the Signs of the Times*, New York: Scribner, 1946.

Niederaver, George. "The Gift of Laughter." *New Catholic World*, January-February 1978, pp. 36-37. Laughter as recognition and acceptance of the gaps in faith; short article, but good.

Nieting, Lorenz. "Humor in the New Testament." *Dialog*, Summer 1983, pp. 168-170. General look at humor and its dynamics in the New Testament.

Niklaus, Thelma. *Harlequin Phoenix, or the Rise and Fall of a Bergamack Rogue*. London: The Bodley Head, 1956.

Nobleman, Roberta. *Mime and Masks*. Conn: New Play Books, 1979.

Nolan, Joseph T. "Prayer for Having a Good Time." *1979 Clown, Mime, Puppet and Dance Workbook*, 1 page.

Nouwen, Henri, J.M. *Clowning in Rome: Reflections on Solitude, Celibacy, Prayer, and Contemplation*. Garden City: Image Books,

1979. The introduction makes the connection between living simple, humble Christian lives and living as clowns on the edges of the main acts of life.

_____. *Reaching Out: The Three Movements of Spiritual Life.* Garden City: Doubleday and Company. Helpful with therapeutic clowning.

Nutt, Grady. "Humor, Story and Communication." *Catalyst Cassettes,* (12 minutes), January 1976, No. 1.

Nye, Robert. "Laughter is a Serious Subject." *Christian Science Monitor,* September 30, 1975.

Oakland Tribune. "Clowning Mime Troupes Liven the Church Scenario." May 9, 1981, 1 page.

O'Collins, Gerald. "Christian Laughter." *America,* March 18, 1972, p. 294. Genuine laughter, not gloom, should draw the lines on one's face.

*_____. *What are They Saying About Jesus?* New York: Paulist Press, 1978. What Jesus did and did not talk about. See the Appendix on "The Imagination of Jesus."

O'Flaherty, Terrence. "Good, Innocent Fun with a Joyful Clown," (Bill Irwin), *San Francisco Chronicle,* February 7, 1983.

O'Grady, Michael, and Manno, Bruno V. "Send in the Clowns: Theory and Practice in Adult Faith Development." *The Living Light,* Vol. 16, No. 4, pp. 469-479.

Ong, Walter. "Wit and Mystery: A Revaluation in Medieval Latin Hymnody, the Barbarian Within." pp. 88-130.

Orsy, Ladislas M. "In Praise of Fools." *America,* March 14, 1970, p. 276. Connects fools and comtemplatives as needed observers and commentators of society.

Ossman, G. "Between the Lines: Sts. Peter and Paul and Humor." *Marist,* September-October 1964, pp. 32-35.

Ortegel, Adelaide. "Mime: The Silence that Shouts." *Modern Liturgy,* September/October 1980, p. 10. Guidelines for miming; sets the framework for mime in silence; good ideas for creations for worship.

Parabola Magazine. A magazine dedicated to the study of myth and tradition. $18 a year; good investment. Write to Subscription Department, 150 5th Avenue, New York, New York, 10011. The February 1979 issue is devoted to Fools and Tricksters. Some back issues can be purchased.

Parabola. "Lie and Glorious Adjective: An Interview with Peter

Brook." *Parabola*, Summer 1981, pp. 60-73. The movie director speaks on masks and images.

_____. "Through a Glass, Darkly." *Parabola*, Summer 1981, pp. 40-42. Quotes on masks and metaphor.

Parker, Stewart. *Spokesong*. New York: Samuel French, Inc, 1979, 1980.

Parrill, Lloyd. "Concept of Humor in the Pseudonymous Works of Soren Kierkegaard." *The Drew Gateway*, 1975-1976, pp. 116-117.

Parrott, Bob W. "Ontology of Humor: A Basis for Biblical Exegesis." *Perkins School of Theology Journal*, Fall 1978, pp. 14-34.

Patka, Frederick. *The Clowns*. Albany: Magi Books. Modern adults in their world of make-believe.

Paul, Eileen. "Liturgy as an Act of Imagination." *Liturgy*, February 1977, pp. 18-21. How liturgy can use imagination to provide a glimpse of a different way of looking at life.

Payne, Pierre Stephan Robert. *The Great God Pan*. New York: Hermitage House, 1952. A biography of Chaplin.

Pawlikowshi-Cholewa, Harald von. *Le Mime Marcel Marceau*. Hamburg: J.M. Hoeppner, 1955. In German, French, English, Italian, and Spanish.

Pearce, Richard. *Stages of the Clown: Perspectives on Modern Fiction from Dostoyevsky to Brecht.* Preface by Harry T. Moore. Illinois: Southern Illinois University Press, 1970.

Pelton, Robert D. *The Trickster in West Africa: Sacred Irony and Myth Delight.* Berkeley: University of California Press, 1980.

Petchul, Sherry. "A Puppet Show with no Strings Attached." *Christian Science Monitor*. On the Caravan Theater and its Native American stories.

Phipps, Carol J. "Suggestions for Clowning for Christ." *1982 Clown, Mime, Puppet and Dance Workbook*, 3 pages.

Pintauro. *One Circus, Three Rings, Forever and Ever, Hooray.*

Pitt, Leonard. "Mask Techniques for the Actor." *San Francisco Theatre*, Winter 1977, pp. 81-83.

_____. *Mime and Movement.* by Leonard Pitt, 1977. Includes "An Experience in Bali," "Mime and Pantomime," "Form and Technique," "The Beginnings and the Ends of a Movement," and "Mask Technique for the Actor."

Podolsky, Edward. "Rx: Hearty Laughter." *Commonweal*, March 24, 1939, pp. 601-602. On Dr. Pierre Vachet, and the therapy of humor.

Polhill, John B. "Wisdom of God and Factionalism: First Corninthians 1-4." *Review and Exposition*, Summer 1983, pp. 325-339. On Paul's comment on the foolishness of God in the text.

Portaro, Sam. "Holiness and Hilarity: the Reverent Irreverence of Mrk Twain." *Criterion*, Spring 1983, pp. 22-25. A perceptive examination of Twain and his perceptions of organized religion. In a way Twain was an early version of Lenny Bruce; or visa versa.

Potthoff, Harvey H. "Humor and Religious Faith." *American Theological Librarians Association Proceedings*, 1980, pp. 74-80.

Price, Ann F. "A Clown." *1980 Clown, Mime, Puppet and Dance Workbook*, 2 pages. Poem about a man seeming a clown for the first time from his hospital bed, and really opening up to life again.

Pulver, Charles R. "Clown Mass Criticized by Priests, Nuns." *The Wanderer*, September 1981, pp. 1, 8.

Radin, Paul. *The Trickster: A Study in American Indian Mythology.* New York: Schocken Books, 1972. An important study on the teickster.

Rahner, Hugo. "Eutrapelia: A Forgotten Virtue." in *Holy Laughter*, ed. by Conrad Hyers; New York: Seabury Press, 1969, pp. 185-197. On jesting with good taste, from *Man at Play*, by Rahner, New York: Herder and Herder, 1965.

————————. *Man At Play.* New York: Herder and Herder, 1967. On the theology of play and recreation.

Redding, David A. "God Made Me To Laugh." *Christianity Today*, July 6, 1962, pp. 3-4.

Reid, Clyde. *Celebrate the Temporary.*

Reilly, P.P. "It is to Laugh." *Homiletic and Pastoral Review*, April 1953, pp. 632-633.

Reines, Chaim W. "Laughter in Biblical and Rabbinic Literature." *Judaism*, Spring 1972, pp. 176-183.

*Remington, Leo. "Clowning in Liturgy by 'Tug'." *Modern Liturgy*, September/October 1980, p. 45. Good introduction to the Clown Eucharist service: gentle, aimed at where many congregations are.

————————. "The Love Plant." *1980 Clown, Mime, Puppet and Dance Workbook*, 2 pages. A clown routine for a special person or special occasion.

*_____, and Krall, Jack. "A Clown Eucharist Service." *Modern Liturgy*, September/October 1980, pp. 46-47. Also in the *1979 Clown, Mime, Puppet and Dance Workbook*. With directions, music, timing, firm and benediction information for putting the service on.

Rice, Charles L. *Interpretation and Imagination*. Philadelphia: Fortran Press, 1970. A nice, little volume from the Preacher's Paperback Library; on how to draw help from non-Biblical material for preaching.

Rickard, Wayne. "An Island of Love." *1982 Clown, Mime, Puppet and Dance Workbook*, 3 pages. On heart-to-heart touching in clowning.

Ridington, Robin. "Mirrors and Masks." *Parabola*, November 1979, pp. 84-90. A modern presentation of shanism.

Risley, M. "Litanies and Limericks." *Catholic Library World*, March 1951, pp. 170-173.

*Rolfe, Bari. *Behind the Mask*. Oakland: Persona Books, 1977. A good introduction to mask work.

_____. *Commedia dell 'Arte: A Scene Study Book*. Oakland: Persona Books, 1977.

_____. "Mask, Mime, amd Mummenschanz," interview. *Mime Journal*, No. 2, Thomas Leabhart, ed. Univ. of Arkansas, Fayetteville, 1975.

_____. "Mime in America; A Survey." *Mime Journal*, No. 1, 1974, pp. 2-12.

_____. ed. *Mimes on Miming: Writings on the Art of Mime*. Los Angeles: Panjadrum Books, 1979. Short selections by or about mimes, including Decroux Barrault, Marceau, Popov, Dimitri, Keaton, Mummenschanz, Avital, and Shields.

*Roskies, David G. "Sholem Aleichem and Others: Laughing Off the Trauma of History." *Prooftexts*, January 1982, pp. 53-77. Deals with the use of humor as a defense against persecution, using the Jewish experience in the 20th century as an example.

Roston, Leo. *The Joys of Yiddish*. New York: Pocket Books, 1968.

Roundtable discussion on humor and religion: transcript of the TV program. *Catholic Messenger*, November 7, 1963, p. 5.

Russel, E. *Paranomasia and Kindred Phenomena in the New Testament*.

Russell, Jim. "Resume of Clown Make-up Products." *1980 Clown, Mime, Puppetand Dance Workbook*, 3 pages.

_____. "Selecting Balloons for Balloon Sculpturing." *1980 Clown, Mime, Puppet and Dance Work-book.*

Ryan, J. "Church Art and Artitecture: On Being a Catholic Cart-tonist." *Clergy Review*, April 1977, pp. 142-145. On the difficulty of being funny, relevant, correct, and appreciated.

Ryan, Wendy. "It's a New Day." *Today's American Baptist*, May 1981, pp. 15-17. Using clowning with retarded people at Grotonwood Camp.

Salamone, Frank. "Religion as Play: Bori, a Friendly Witch-doctor." *Journal of Religion in Africa*, 1975, pp. 201-211.

Saler, Benson. "A Look at Ritual." *Liturgy*, January 1973, pp. 10-18. Deals with how anthropologists look at ritual, and its function with societies.

Saliers, Don E. "Faith and the Comic Eye; Religious Gleanings from Comic Vision in Some Recent Fiction." *Andover Newton Quarterly*, March 1973, pp, 259-276.

Samra, Cal. "I'd Like to Say: Jesus Put on a Happy Face!" *St. Anthony Messenger*, September 1983, pp. 24-27.

_____. *The Joyful Christ: The Healing Power of Humor.* San Francisco: Harper and Row, 1985.

Sanders, Toby. *How to be a Complete Clown.* New York: Stein and Day, 1978. Good book on all kinds of clowns. It is less theoretical than Towsen's *Clowns.* The emphasis is on the pratical applications.

*Saward, John. "The Fool for Christ'a Sake in Monasticism, East and West." *Cistercian Studies*, 29, 1976, pp. 48-80. Very good overview of the place of Holy Fools within the organized structure of the Orthodox Christian Churches. It is a short version of his later work, *Perfect Fools.*

*_____. *Perfect Fools: Folly for Christ's Sake in Catholic and Orthodox Spirituality.* Oxford: Oxford University Press, 1980. The first half of the book deals in detail with the history of holy fools in Russia, Greece, and Ireland; while the second half focuses in on the people within 17th century fooldom; this is an expansion of his 1976 article.

Sawyer, Ruth. *The Way of the Stryteller.* New York: Viking Press, 1962. A classic on the theory and practice of storytelling.

Schall, James V. "The Papacy and Humour."*Month*, September

1969, pp. 110-120. Good representation on sociology and humor versus somberness.

*Schechner, Richard and Mady Schuman, eds. *Ritual, Play and Performance: Readings in the Social Sciences and Theatre.* New York: Seabury Press, 1976. It has chapters by a wide variety of respected people: Turner, Huizinga, Bateson, Lorenz, Goodall, etc. They talk about shamnism, meditation, rites, ceremonies, performances, play, ethology, and rituals.

Schiffers, Norbert. "The Humor of John XXIII," in *Theology of Joy,* edited by Metz and Jossua, New York: Herder and Herder, 1974, pp. 126-133. Good presentation of how Pope John used humor to humanize situation while he was pope.

Schimel, Mary Aileen. "Holidays and Wholly Dazed." *Bear and Company,* Vol. 1, No. 5, p. 10. Provides a brief context for Ken Feit.

_____. "Praymate of the Month." *Bear and Company,* Vol. 1, No. 5, pp. 11-12. On Ken Feit.

Scott, Nathan, Jr. "The Bias of Comedy and the Narro Escape Into Faith." ed. by Conrad Hyers; New York: Seabury Press, 1969, pp. 45-74. On comedy and literature, secular theories, and the ties between tragedy and comedy; from *The Christian Scholar,* Spring 1961, pp. 9-39. Presents the basic function og the comic person to be a kind of icon of the human actuality. Also in *The Broken Center: Studies in the Theological Horizon of Modern Literature.* New Haven: Yale University Press, 1966.

*Sekaquaptewa, Emory. "One More Smile for a Hopi Clown." *Parabola,* February 1979, pp. 6-9. Good insights into the theology of clowning for the Hopi.

Senelick, Laurence. *A Cavalcade of Clowns.* San Francisco: Bellerophon Books, 1977.

Sexson, Lynda. "Craftsman of Chaos." *Parabola,* February 1979, pp. 25-33. On the role of the fool of the Tarot.

*Shaffer, Floyd. "The Clown — Another Fool for Christ's Sake." *Military Chaplains' Review,* Fort Wadsworth, Staten Island, New York: U.S. Army, pp. 15-22. This article is basically the same as his "God Loves Clowns," although there is additional information here.

*_____. "Clowns in Worship? What Next?" *Modern Liturgy,* August 1981, pp. 6-7. Has some important liturgical clowning ideas, such as clowning is a delivery system, not a performance.

*_____. "Faith and Fantasy." *Thesis Theological Cassette.* March 1977, side two. Nice overview on the theology of clowning.

**   , and Sewell, Penne. *Clown Ministry*, Loveland, Co: Group Books, 1984, 112 pages. A how-to book, with ideas, and skits for learning or teaching.

_____. "Fools for Christ — Clowns for Christ." *1981 Clown, Mime, Puppet and Dance Workbook*, 5 pages. It has the etymology and rules for clowning, qith some aids for developing your own clown.

*_____. "God Loves Clowns." *The Other Side*, December 1979, pp. 17-25; (300 W. Apsley St., Philadelphia, PA 19144). Excellent overview of the whole Christian clowning scene. God and esus had a sense of humor.

**   . *If I Were a Clown*. Minneapolis: Augsburg Publishing, 1984, 128 pages. Shaffer's personal experiences and reflections from his clown ministry; with make-up and skit ideas. A valuable resource from an inside "feel" of what it means to be a clown.

*Shea, John. *Stories of God: An Unauthorized Biography*. Chicago: Thomas More Press, 1978. A work of narrative theology; how theology has its roots in the lives of people; works with the idea that God loves stories.

Shedlock, Marie. *Art of the Storyteller*. New York: Dover Books, 1951. A classic on the dynamics of telling stories.

Sheen, Bp. F.J. "Divine Sense of Humor." *Catholic World*, April 1954, pp. 1-5. As Catholics, we should be happy, not gloomy.

Sheerin, John B. "God, Man and the Clowns." *Homiletic and Pastoral Review*, August 1952, pp. 965-969.

_____. "Let's Have Some Humor." *Catholic World*, April 1954, pp. 1-5. As Christians, we should be happy, not gloomy.

Shepard, Richard. *Mime: The Technique of Silence: An Illustrated Workbook*. Drama Book Specialists, 1971.

Sherwood, Robert. *Here We Are Again: Recollections of an Old Circus Clown*. Indianapolis: Bobbs-Merrill Co, 1926.

Shields, Robert. *Mime in Our Time*. San Francisco: Get the Hook Productions, 1972.

Short, Robert L. *The Gospel According to Peanuts*. Atlanta: John Knox Press, 1965. Examines in a fun way the theology present in the Peanut comic strip by Charles Schulz.

_____. *The Parables of Peanuts*. New York: Harper and Row, 1968. Cintinues the study begun with the Gospel According to ....

Simpson, Mona. "Mime: The Art of Silence." *The Daily Californian*, May 23, 1980, p. 9. An historical overview of mime.

Smith, Morton. *Jesus the Magician*. San Francisco: Harper and Row, 1978. Explores the notion that there is a little odor of snake oil around Jesus. A critical historical look at magicians and their world in the time of Jesus, and hiw Jesus may have borrowed from them.

*Smith, Robert T. "World's Smallest Circus May Be Largest Ministry." *Minneapolis Tribune*, March 19, 1980, pp. 1B, 3B. A report on Nick Webber's Royal Lichenstein Quarter-ring Circus, and its ministry.

Smith, William Austin. "The Use of the Comic Spirit in Religion. *Atlantic Monthly*, August 1911, p. 188.

Solle, Dorothee, and Fulbert Steffensky. "Christianity as Joy in Sects and Fringe Groups." in *Theology of Joy*, edited by Metz and Jossua, New York: Herder and Herder, 1974, pp. 113-125. How the joy of having to suffer for a cause contributes to believing in the great joy of Christ.

Sparough, J. Michael. "Mime: Pathway to Prayer." *Modern Liturgy*, September/October 1980, pp. 42-43. On using Ignatious's exercises and imagination to enter into Bible stories.

Speaight, George. *The Book of Clowns*. New York: Macmillan Pub. Co, 1980.

_____. *Punch and Judy: A History*. rev. ed. London: Studio Vista, 1970. History of English puppet theater.

*Spolin, Viola. *Improvisation for the Theater: A Handbook of Teaching and Directing Techniques*. Northwestern University Press, 1963. Updated with new preface, 1983. Still the best on a neglected subject. Deals with how to help others to unblock spontaneity and creativity.

Stair, Rolland, CSC 1932-1981. "Be a Clown." *Our Sunday Visitor Magazine*, June 1981, p. 16.

Steere, David. "Our Capacity for Sadness and Joy: An Essay on Life Before Death," in *Theology of Joy*, edited by Metz and Jossua, New York: Herder and Herder, 1974, pp. 15-30. On choosing to live fully now, rather than living only to die.

Steinfels, Peter. "No Laughing Matter: Corporate Executives Need Humor." *Commonweal*, July 8, 1977, p. 434. On Robert Orben's work as comedy consultant to business as a sales tactic.

Steinsaltz, Adin. "The Human Image." *Parabola*, Summer 1981, pp. 43, 47. On Judaism, amsks and iconography.

Sterritt, David. "Many-sided Bread and Puppet Man." *Christian Science Monitor*, February 9, 1973, p. 16. On Peter Schumann, director of Vermont's Bread and Puppet Theater.

Stevens Mark. "Comedian School is no Laughing Matter." *Christian Science Monitor*.

*Stinespring, W.F. "Humor." *The Interpreters Dictionary of the Bible*, Vol. E-J, pp. 660-662.

* _____. "Irony and Satire." *The Interpreters Dictionary of the Bible*, Vol. E-J, pp. 726-728.

Stolzenberg, Mark. *Clown for Circus and Stage*. New York: Sterling Publishing Company, 1981.

_____. *Exploring Mime*. New York: Sterling Publishing Company, 1979.

Stonebruner, Tony, ed. (Seminar on) *Parable, Myth and Language*. Cambridge: Church Society for College Work, 1968. Cintributors include Stephen Crites, Robert Duncan, Robert Funk, Samuel Laeuchli, Denise Levertov, James Robinson, Hollis Summers, Amos Wilder, Philip Zabriskie.

Strange, Marian. "God and Laughter." *Worship*, January 1971, pp. 2-12.

Strelak, Richard, and Sherman, Marty. *Clown Hits and Skits*. Downers Grove: Contemporary Drama Service, 1981. Bare Bone skit ideas.

*Sugg, Joyce. "Did Newman Have a Sense of Humor?" *Clergy Review*, March 1983, pp. 100-104. Confronts and disputes the general image of a serious Newman; presents his quiet wit and humor.

Suhor, M. "Be a Clown: Developing a Sense of Humor." *Queen's Work*, April 1963, pp. 6-8.

Sullivan, J. Leo. "Laughter is a Strong Armour." *Ave Maria*, May 26, 1951, pp. 655-657. About humor seeing below the surface of things, and finding God's strength.

Surface, Maxine. "Lord, I Want to be a Clown." *1980 Clown, Mime, Puppet and Dance Workbook*, 1 page. A clown prayer that is better than the "Prayer of a Clown."

Svoboda, Mary Melannie. "Humor: A Kindly Contemplation." *Sisters Tiday*, October 1976, pp. 73-76. How a loss of humor may result in a loss of vocations; humor as what enables different people to live together as a cloister.

Swabey, Marie Taylor (Collins). *Comic Laughter: A Philosophical*

Essay. New Have: Yale University Press, 1932. A solid book on fools during this period.

Swain, Barbara. *Fools and Folly During the Middle Ages and the Renaissance.* New York: Columbia University Press, 1932. A solid book on fools during this period.

Sypher, Wylie, ed. *Comedy: An Essay on Comedy by George Meredith. "Laughter" by Henri Bergson.* New York: Doubleday and Co. 1956. Sypher also has an essay on "The Meaning of Comedy" in the Appendix.

Syrkin, Alexander Y. "On the Behavior of the "Fool for Christ'a Sake." *History of Religions,* November 1982, pp. 150-171. A nice presentation, read in conjunction with Saward's article.

Tafoya, Terry. "Dancing with Dash-kayah: the Mask of the Cannibal Woman." *Parabola,* Summer 1981, pp. 6-11. On transformations.

Tannenbaum, Mac. "Humor in the Talmud." in *Theology of Joy,* edited by Metz and Jossua, New York: Herder and Herder, 1974, pp. 141-150. Abour how rabbis denounce frivolity, but celebrate the healthy psychology of laughter.

Taylor, Margaret, and Adams, Doug. "Humor in Liturgical Music and Dance." *Modern Liturgy,* December/January 1979, p. 36.

Taylor, Nora E. "When Marcel Marceau Speaks . . ." *Christian Science Monitor.*

Taylor, Robert Lewis. *Center Ring: the People of the Circus.* New York: Doubleday and Co, 1956. An illustrated edition on the performers.

_____. *W.C. Fields: His Follies and Fortunes.* Garden City: Doubleday and Co., 1949.

*Tedlock, Barbara. "Boundaries of Belief." *Parabola,* February 1979, pp. 70-77. Good insights into the Zuni Indian clowns of New Mexico; how shock is important for opening the people up to new possibilities.

Tietze-Conrat, Erica. *Dwarfs and Jesters in Art.* London: Phaidon Press, 1957. 90 illustrations discussed.

Timmerman, John. "Tragicomedy and Saving Grace." *Christian Century,* November 26, 1975, pp. 1076-1080.

Towne, Anthony. *Excerpts from the Diaries of the Late God.* New York: Harper and Row.

*Towsen, John H. *Clowns: A Panoramic History.* New York: Hawthorn Books, 1976. The definitive book on secular clowns and fools throughout history. The best I have found.

Trambling, Kathy. "102 Gifts." *1980 Clown, Mime, Puppet and Dance Workbook*, 1 page. Thoughtful, loving gifts that clowns, or anyone, can give to people; creative.

Trolin, Clif. "Celebrating the Sabbath With Mime." *Modern Liturgy*, September/October 1980, p. 44. How visualizations can be a preparation for the service.

*Trueblood, Elton. *The Humor of Christ*. New York: Harper and Row, 1964. A good beeok for exposing people to the notion that Jesus maybe smiled once in a while.

——————————. "The Humor of Christ." in *Holy Laughter*, ed. by Conrad Hyers; New York: Seabury Press, 1969, pp. 166-184. Biblical Study; from "A Neglected Aspect" in *The Humor of Christ*. New York: Harper and Row, 1964.

Tucker, Janet. "Ideas for Using Your Clown in a Church Setting." *1982 Clown, Mime, Puppet and Dance Workbook*, 1 page.

Twigg-Porter, George. "Freedom to Laugh." *Linacre Quarterly*, August 1968, pp. 223-224.

Ulanov, Barry. "Rhetoric of Christian Comedy." in *Holy Laughter*, ed. by Conrad Hyers; New York: Seabury Press, 1969, pp. 103-122. On theology and literature; from *Literature as Christian Comedy*. W. Hartford: St. Joseph's College, 1962.

Urdahl, Richard. *Plays for Clowns in Christ: Four Short Plays for the Fun of Playing*. Philadelphia: Fortress Press, 1973. It's Okay.

*Vannorsdall, John. "Humor as Content and Device in Preaching." *Dialog*, Summer 1983, pp. 187-190. Focuses on a Buechner talk on the "Gospel as Comedy," and cautions against using humor in preaching just to get a laugh, if it does not preach the gospel.

Vecsey, Christopher. "The Exception Who Proves the Rules: Ananse the Akan Trickster." *Journal of Religion in Africa*, 1981, pp. 161-177.

Velez, Colleen. "Clowning." *Catechist*, January 1984, pp. 24-25. An account of clowning for First Eucharist.

Verney, Peter. *Here Comes the Circus*. New York and London: Paddington Press, 1978. Nice picturebook. Chapter 5 is on clowns, pp. 156-179.

Verriest-LeFert, Guy and Jeanne. *Marcel Marceau ou L aventure du Silence*, interview with Marceau. Paris: Descleau de Broumer, 1974. Translated by Bari Rolfe, and revised by Marceau.

Via, Dan Otto. *Kerygma and Comedy in the New Testament: A*

Structuralist Approach to Hermeneutics. Philadelohia: Fortran Press, 1975.

_____. *The Parables: Their Literary and Existential Dimension.* Philadelphia: Fortran Press, 1967.

Von Rad, Gerhard. *The Message of the Prophets.* New York: Harper and Row, 1962.

Vos, Nelvin. *The drama of Comedy: Victim and Victor.* Atlanta: John Knox Press, 1966. Comic victor of Wilder, Comic victim of Ionesco, Comic victim-victor of Fry, and the meeting of comedy and the Christian faith.

_____. *For God's Sake Laugh.* Atlanta: John Knox Press, 1967.

Wagoner, Walter D. *Bittersweet Grace.* World. A treasury of 20th century religious satire.

_____. "A Godly Sense of Humor." *Christian Century.*

Walker, Jacqulyn E. "Fleshing Out The Word." *Modern Liturgy,* September/October 1980, pp. 18-19.

Wallace, John. "Street Clowning." Unpublished article on how to lead a group through a street clowning experience, 1984.

_____. *Why Don't we Do-It-In the Street?* Bethlehem: Hamilton Hall Press, 1984. A decent study of street clowning in the UCC and Moravian traditions.

Wallis, Ernest. *Wit and Wisdom of the Christian Fathers of Egypt: The Syrian Version of the Apophthegmata Patrum.* Compiled by Anan Isho and translated by Wallis. Oxford University Press; reprinted by AMS Press, 1934 edition.

Walsh, Chad. "On Being With It: An Afterward." in *Holy Laughter,* edited by Conrad Hyers; New York: Seabury Press, 1969, pp. 241-251. On the spirit of the comic.

Walsh, Edward R. "The Lord Loves Laughter." *Ligourian,* March 1981, pp. 44-49. A large secular overview.

_____. "Papal Indulgencies: Wit and Humor in the Vtican." *Ligourian,* February 1983, pp. 14-16. Light anecdotes from experiences in the Vatican.

Watts, Alan. *Behold the Spirit: A Study in the Necessity of Mystical Religion.* New York: Pantheon, 1947, esp. pp. 175-181. Talks about seeing God as playful, and valuing frivolous humor.

*Weber, Nick. Article by Valene Harper. "Priest's Little Big Show

Blends Circus, Religion." *National Catholic Reporter*, November 23, 1973, pp. 1, 15. Good presentation of Weber's quarter-ring circus ministry.

*_____. Article by Robert T. Smith. "World's Smallest Circus May be Largest Ministry." *Minneapolis Tribune*, March 19, 1980, pp. 1B, 3B. A report on Weber's circus, and its ministry.

_____. Article by J. Wintz. "Hold Fast to Dreams: Nick Weber SJ and his Sidewalk Circus." *Saint Anthony*, July 1974, pp. 28-37.

Weber, Peter. "A Christian Activist Talks About Comedy and Social Justice." *On the Edge Newsletter*, 2 pages.

_____. "To Be the Clown is to Profess the Resurrection." *The Other Side*, December 1979, pp. 20-21. A Christian activist looks at comedy and social justice.

*Wedge, Florence. "King's Jesters: Saints." *Sign*, August 1956, p. 17. A nice, quick summary of the saints and their humor.

Weidman, Judy. "Cleric Clown Finds More Joyous Christianity." *The United Methodist Reporter*, January 4, 1974, p. 3. On Rev. Bill Pechsm and his ministry to hospitals and nursing homes.

Wells, Joel. "A God Who Laughs." *AD*. February 1982, pp. 26-27. Reprinted from *Notre Dame Magazine*. About how hard it is for many Christians to laugh at religious jokes, and at general humor.

_____. "The Laugh That Failed." *U.S. Catholic*, May 1971, p. 40.

*Welsford, Enid. *The Fool: His Social and Literary History.* Gloucester: Peter Smith. 1966 reprint of the 1935 Faber abd Faber original. Excellent overview.

Welsh, W.A. "Homo Ridens: Preliminary Consideration of Some Aspects of Human Laughter." *Lexington Theological Quarterly*, October 1967, pp. 95-103.

West, Morris. *The Clowns of God.* Bantam Books, 1981. Although the mentally-retarded are called the clowns in this novel, as role-models, the unnamed clowns — Christians — are held up for believing in the folly of the cross as a way to disarm the nuclear madness.

Whedbee, William. "Comedy of Job." *Semeia*, 1977, pp. 1-39.

Whelan, L.F. "Virtue of Humor." *Homiletic and Pastoral Review*, June 1957, pp. 38-40.

Wiesel, Elie. *Souls on Fire.* New York: Random House, 1972.

Wilde, Larry. *The Great Comedians Talk About Comedy.* New York: Citadel Press, 1968. Interviews with 16 comedians.

_____. *How the Great Comedy Writers Create Laughter.* Chicago: Nelson Hall, 1976.

Wiley, Jack. *Basic Circus Skills.* Harrisburg, PA: Stackpole Books, 1974. How to develop 17 basic circus skills.

*Wilhelm, Roberta Bela. "How Tales are Told." *Liturgy,* May 1974, pp. 3-8. On the place of storytelling within liturgy.

_____. "The Liturgist as Story Teller." *Modern Liturgy,* November/December 1976, pp. 26-27. On the preparation and application of telling stories.

* _____. "Storytelling." (columes) *Liturgy,* generally speaking each issue, from 1974 to 1978. Good hints on story telling, and the dynamics involved.

_____. *Storytelling as a Religious Art Form for Contemporary Christianity.* Unpublished dissertation, Graduate Theological Union Library, 1976. On educators workshop on storytelling, On educators workshop on storytelling, an illustrated story, and on guided mythmaking.

Willeford, William. *The Fool and His Scepter: A Study in Clowns and Jesters and Their Audiences.* Illinois: Northwestern University Press, 1969. Focus on the fool actor and the interactions with the audience.

Williams, James G. "Comedy of Jacob: A Literary Study." *Journal of the American Academy of Religion,* June 1978, p. 208.

Williams, Jay. *The School for Sillies* Parents Magazine Press, 1969.

*Williams, Julia A, and Griener, Stephen G. "Therapeutic Clowning as a Treatment Modality." *1980 Clown, Mime, Puppet and Dance Workbook,* 4 pages. The difference between circus clowning and therapeutic clowning; how the barrier between the adult world and the fantasy/child world is transcended.

Williams, Paul, V. ed. *The Fool and the Trickster: STudies in Honor of Enid Welsford.* New Jersey: Rowman and Littlefield, 1979.

Winn, Steven. "Delightful Inventions From a Clown." (Geoff Hoyle), *San Francisco Chronicle,* August 11, 1983.

*Winton-Henry, Cynthia. "Improvisation: Making Way for an Extraordinary Ordinary Time." *Modern Liturgy,* Vol. 11, No. 3, pp. 4-5. Stresses that improv is both an art form and a way of life. Points out that there is tremendous creativity available to anyone at any moment. Good article.

Wintz, J. "Hold Fast to Dreams: Nick Weber SJ and his Side-walk Circus." *Saint Anthony*, July 1974, pp. 28-37.

Wise, Naomi. "Monty Python: They Kid You Not." *East Bay Express.*

Wisse, Ruth R. *The Schlemiel as Modern Hero.* Chicago: University of Chicago Press, 1071. Traces the Schlemiel (fool) through Jewish literature from culture to culture.

Wolferman, Tom. "The Mime Menace: How to Spot It. What to Do About It." *East Bay Express*, March 28, 1980, pp. 1, 3. How to tell safe mimes from the dangerous ones.

Woodward, Tom. *Turning Things Upside Down: a Theological Workbook.* Seabury Press. A nice introduction to Christian Theology.

*_____. "Israel and the Clown." *Clown, Mime, Puppet and Dance Workbook*, 9 pages. Good overview of clowning, with a nice collection of theoughts; a lot of material on how clowns can help us laugh at ourselves and our humanness.

_____. "Street Liturgy." *Modern Liturgy*, August 1981, p. 32. A sample clown routine for the street.

Wordeman, Martha. "Catechists and Children Can Be Clowns for Christ." *Religious Teacher's Journal*, January 1981, pp. 7-8.

_____. "Clowns for Christ." *Religion Teachers Journal*, January 1981, pp. 7-8.

Worgul, George S. Jr. "Symbols and Imagination." *Modern Liturgy*, February 1984, pp. 24-25. How liturgy needs symbols and imagination for it to be worship.

Wright, John H. "God's Story in our Lives." *Modern Liturgy*, November/December 1976, p. 13.

Yancey, Philip. "How Dirty Jokes and the Fear of Death Prove There is a Heaven." *Christianity Today*, March 2, 1984, p. 28.

Zenner, Edward. "Mime Stations of the Cross." *Modern Liturgy*, March 1978, pp. 24-25.

Ziolkowski, Theodore. *Fictional Transfigurations of Jesus.* Princeton: Princeton University Press, 1972. Traces the portrayals of Jesus in literature in the last 100 years.

Zone, Ray. "Inner Faces." *Parabola*, Summer 1981, pp. 22-29. Myth and masks in horror films, murder mysteries, and comic books. An interesting combination.

*Zucker, Wolfgang M. "The Clown as the Lord of Disorder." *Theology Today*, October 1967, pp. 306-317. Also in *Holy Laughter*, edited by Conrad Hyers. New York: Seabury Press, 1969, pp. 75-88. Nice overview of clowning; with d good insights into the place of disorder in the Church.

Zuesse, Evan M. "Divination and Deity in African Religions." *History of Religion*, November 1975, pp. 158-182.

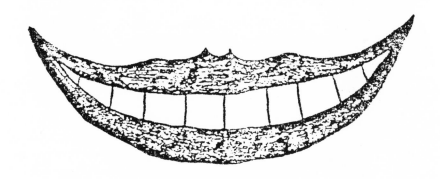

Clowns are pegs used to hang circuses on.
—Phineas T. Barnum

Credo quia absurdum:
I believe because it
it is absurd.

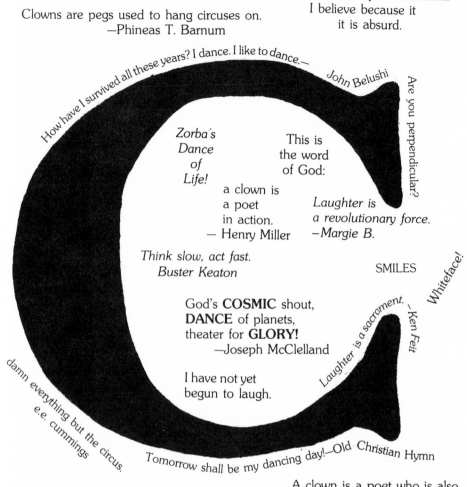

How have I survived all these years? I dance. I like to dance.— John Belushi

Are you perpendicular?

Zorba's
Dance
of
Life!

This is
the word
of God:

a clown is
a poet
in action.
— Henry Miller

Laughter is
a revolutionary force.
—Margie B.

Think slow, act fast.
Buster Keaton

SMILES

Whiteface!

God's **COSMIC** shout,
DANCE of planets,
theater for **GLORY!**
—Joseph McClelland

Laughter is a sacrament. —Ken Feit

I have not yet
begun to laugh.

damn everything but the circus.
e.e. cummings

Tomorrow shall be my dancing day!—Old Christian Hymn

We shall be clowns together.
—Thomas Merton

A clown is a poet who is also
an orangutang.—Steve Linser

The test of a good religion
is whether you can make a joke about it.
—G.K. Chesterton

Reading List

On Christian Clowning and Related Subjects
(see the Annotated Bibliography for details)

General Christian Clowning

Ken Feit, "The Priestly Fool"
Patrick Forbes, "Gospel Fool"
Kenneth Hamilton, "Laughter and Vision"
Conrad Hyers, *The Comic Vision and the*   *Christian Faith*
Tim Kehl, "The Theology of Clowning"
Floyd Shaffer, *If I Were a Clown*

General Secular Clowning

Paul Bouissae, *Circus and Culture: A Semiotic Approach*
Paul Cline, *Fools, Clowns and Jesters*
Barbara Swain, *Fools and Folly During the Middle Ages and the Renaissance*
John Towsen, *Clowns*
Enid Welsford, *The Fool: His Social and Literary History*
William Willeford, *The Fool and his Scepter*

A Clowning Orientation

Frederick Buechner, *Peculiar Treasures: A Biblical Who's Who; Telling the Truth: The Gospel as Tragedy, Comedy, and Fairy Tale; Wishful Thinking: A Theological ABC*
Harvey Cox, *The Feast of Fools: A Theological Essay on Festivity and Fantasy*
Nikos Kazantzakis, *Zorba the Greek*
Sam Keen, *Apology for Wonder To a Dancing God*
Joseph McLelland, *The Clown and the Crocodile*
Metz and Jossua, *Theology of Joy*
Elton Trueblood, *ThHumor of Christ*

Mime

Samuel Avital, *Mime Workbook: Le Center du Silence*
Etienne Decroux, *Words on Mime*
Ken Feit, "In Praise of Hands"
Michael Moynahan, "Discovering God's Gift of Humor Through Liturgical Mime"; "Mime for the Beginner"; "Mime and Worship"
Bari Rolfe, *Mimes on Miming: Writings on the Art of Mime*
Michael Sparough, "Mime: Pathway to Prayer"

Liturgical Clowning

Doug Adams, "Bringing Biblical Humor to Life in Liturgy"
Margie Brown, "Rehearsal in the Center Ring: An Approach to Clown Liturgy"
Patrick Collins, "Liturgy and Imagination"
Jake Empereur, "The Theological Experience"
Ken Feit, "Creative Ministry: A Magical Booklet of Techniques and Experiences"
Michael Moynahan, "Clowns and Sacraments"
Leo Remington, "Clowning in Liturgy by 'Tug' "
Floyd Shaffer, "The Clown — Another Fool for Christ's Sake"; "Clowns in Worship? What Next?"; "Faith and Fantasy"; "God Loves Clowns"; *If I Were a Clown*

Social Action Clowning

Margie Brown, "Clowning Du Jour and Other Entrees for Foolish Feasting"; "Clowning for the Cops"; "Taboo or Not Taboo: That is the Question"
Dorothee Solle, "Christianity as Joy in Sects and Fringe Groups"
Peter Weber, "To be the Clowns to Profess the Resurrection"

Street Clowning

Patricia Campbell, *Passing the Hat*
Tom Woodward, "Street Liturgy"

Therapeutic/Pastoral Clowning

Susan Ambrose, "The Healing Magic of Clowns"
Norman Cousins, *Anatomy of An illnes*
Bob Dvorchak, "Clown Minister Comforts Needy" (Bill Peckham)
Heije Faber, "Second Thoughts on the Minister as a Clown"
Susan Ham, "Who's Afraid of Santa Claus? Overcoming Fear of Costumed Characters: A Therapeutic Recreation Approach"
Seward Hiltner, "The Minister in the Human Circus"
Wolfgang Jilek, *Indian Healing: Shamnaic Ceremonialism* "Love, Laughter, and Healing"
Raymond Moody, *Laugh After Laugh: The Healing Power of Humor*

Humor And Laughter

John Benson, "The Divine Sense of Humor"
Eivind Berggrav, "Humor and Seriousness"
Rick Bernardo, "Or as I Lay Laughing"; "A Serious Meditation on Laughter"
Gerard Bessiere, "Humor — A Theological Attitude?"
Eric Gritsch, "Luthor's Humor: Instrument of Witness"
Kenneth Hamilton, "Laughter and Vision"

Peter Hebblethwaithe, "Clowns for God"
Conrad Hyers, "Christian Humor: Uses and Abuses of Laughter"
Holy Laughter
Harris Kaasa, "Confessions of a Serious-Minded Joker"
John Vannorsdall, "Humor as Content and Device in Preaching"

Improvisation

Patricia deJong, *Improvisation: The Art of Relationship*
Keith Johnstone, *Impro: Improvisation and the Theater*
Viola Spolin, *Improvisation for the Theater: A Handbook of Teaching and Directing Techniques*
Cynthia Winton-Henry, "Improvisation: Making Way for an Extraordinary Ordinary Time"

Bible Studies

Doug Adams, "Bringing to Life the Humor of Jesus' Miracles"; "Playfulness With Paul's Letters"
John Crossman, *Cliffs of Fall: Paradox and Polyvalence in the Parables of Jesus; Raid on the Articulate: Comic Estachology in Jesus and Borges*
Robert Funk, *Language, Hermeneutic, and Word of God*
Joachim Jeremias, *Parables of Jesus*
Elton Trueblood, *The Humor of Christ*

Jewish Foolishness

Martin Buber, *Tales of the Hasidim*
Harold Heifetz, *Zen and Hasidism*
Abraham Heschel, *The Prophets*
David Roskies, "Sholem Aleichem and Others: Laughing Off the Trauma of History"
Leo Rosten, *The Joys of Yiddish*
Adin Steinsaltz, "The Human Image"
Mac Tannenbaum, "Humor in the Talmud"
Ruth Wisse, *The Schlemeil as Modern Hero*

Russian And Greek Orthodox Fools

John Seward, "The Fool for Christ'a Sake in Monasticism, East and West"; *Perfect Fools: Folly for Christ's Sake in Catholic and Orthodox Spirituality*
Alexander Syrkin, "On the Behavior of the Fool for Christ's Sake"

Cross Cultural Clowns

Harold Heifetz, *Zen and Hasidism*
Conrad Hyers, *Zen and the Comic Spirit*
David Leeming, "The Hodja" (Islamic)
Barbara Miller, "Moving Designs of Masked Emotion" (S. India)

Robert Pelton, *The Trickster in West Africa*
John Towsen, *Clowns* (world survey)

Tribal Clowns/Fools/Tricksters/Shamans

D.M. Dooling, "Thw Wisdom of the Contrary: A Conversation with Joseph Epes Brown"
Wolfgang Jilek, *Indian Healing: Shamanic Ceremonialism in the Pacific Northwest Today*
Ron Messer, "A Jungian Interpretation of the Relationship of Culture: Hero and Trickster Figures within Chippewa Mythology"
Robert Pelton, *The Trickster in West Africa: Sacred Irony and Mythic Delight*
Paul Radin, *The Trickster: A Study in American Indian Mythology*
Emory Sekaquaptewa, "One More Smile for a Hopi Clown"
Barbara Tedlock, "Boundaries of Belief" (Zuni Tribe)

Masks

Demorest Davenport, "I Am Not What I Seem" (masks in the animal world)
D.M. Dooling, "Focus"
N. Ross Crumrine, *The Power of Symbols: Masks and Masquerade in the Americans*
Ron Jenkins, "Two-way Mirrors"
J.C.H. King, *Portrait Masks From the NW Coast of America*
Stephen Larsen, "*The Healing Masks*
Claude Levi-Strauss, *The Way of Masks*
Robin Ridington, "Mirrors and Masks"
Ray Zone, "Inner Faces" (masks in horror films, murder mysteries, and comic books)

Metaphor, Ritual, Symbols

David Anderson, "Metaphor, Imagination and the New Religious Era"
Patrick Collins, "Remembering into the Future"
Mircea Eliade, *Myths, Rites, Symbols*
Samuel Miller, "The Clown in Contemporary Art"
Benson Saler, "A Look at Ritual"
Richard Schechner, *Ritual, Play and Performance*
George Worgul, "Symbols and Imagination"

Imagination And Fantasy

Bruno Bettelheim, *The Uses of Enchantment*
Elise Brooke, *Theology and Fantasy*
Patrick Collins, "Liturgy and Imagination"
Harvey Cox, *Feast of Fools: A Theological Essay on Festivity and Fantasy*

Urban Holmes, *Ministry and Imagination*
Charles Rice, *Interpretation and Imagination*

Storytelling

Ken Feit, "Reflections of a Sound Poet"; "Storytelling" (article); "Storytelling" (columns)
J.K. Kadowaki, *Zen and the Bible*
Andrew Lang, his volumes on Fairy Tales
Ruth Sawyer, *The Way of the Storyteller*
Marie Shedlock, *Art of the Storyteller*
Robert Wilhelm, "Storytelling (columns)

Theology Of Story

John Crossman, *The Dark Interval: Towards a Theology of Story*
James McClendon, *Biography as Theology: How Life Stories Can Remake Today's Theology*
Sallie McFague, *Speaking in Parables: A Study in Metaphor and Theology*
John Navone, *Tellers of the Word*
John Shea, *Stories of God: An Unauthorized Biography*

Theology Of Play

Hubert Delaney, "Immortal Diamond"
Johan Huizinga, *Homo Ludens: A Study of the Play Element in Culture*
Robert Johnston, *The Christian at Play*
David Miller, *Gods and Games: Towards a Theology of Play*
Hugo Rahner, *Man at Play*
Frank Salamore, "Religion as Play — Bori, a Friendly Witch-doctor"

Denominations And Humor

Karl Barth: "Joy, Pleasure and Anguish — Thoughts on Barth and Mozart," by Jacques Collette
John XXIII: "The Humor of John XXIII," by Norbert Schiffers
Kierkegaard: "Concept of Humor in the Pseudonymous Works of Soren Kierkegaard," by Lloyd Parrill
Luther: "Luther's Humor: Instrument of Witness," by Eric Gritsch
Thomas More: "Canonization of a Humorist," in *Catholic World*
George Whitefield Through Henry Ward Beecher: *Humor in the American Pulpit*, by Doug Adams

Liminality/Boundary Existence

Jake Empereur, "The Theological Experience"
Patrick Forbes, "Gospel Fool"
Frederick Franck, *Art as a Way: A Return to the Spiritual Roots*
Eileen Paul, "Liturgy as an Act of Imagination"
Thomas Woodward, "Israel and the Clown"

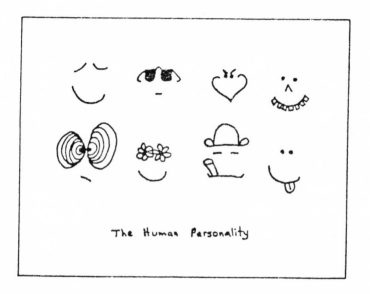

The Human Personality

INDEX

to Clowns, Fools, and Other Assorted Desparados

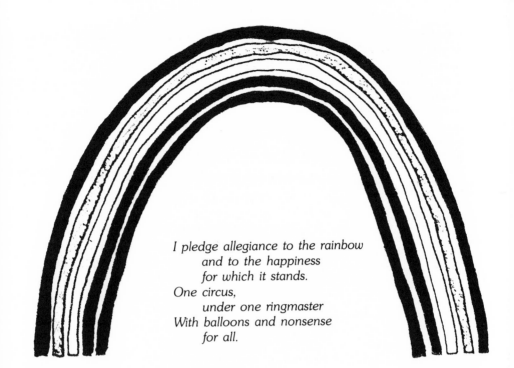

I pledge allegiance to the rainbow
and to the happiness
for which it stands.
One circus,
under one ringmaster
With balloons and nonsense
for all.

Other Clowning Resources From Resource Publications, Inc.

Finding the Clown In Yourself
A Study Experience in Christian Clowning
By Jack Krall and Jan Kalberer

Two active clowns help you get started in clown ministry by helping you find "the little clown" in yourself. Each chapter ends with a Scripture reflection, questions for self examination, and suggestions for further reflection.
Paperbound $7.95
100 pages, 5½"X8½"
ISBN 0-89390-090-7

Stick Stories
By Margie Brown

An entertaining series of stories that lend fresh insight into the Scriptures. Delightful to read and even more fun to act out. Good in the classroom, church, and home.
Paperbound $6.96
64 pages 8½"X11"
ISBN 0-89390-035-4

Available at your bookstore or directly from Resource Publications, Inc., 160 E. Virginia St. #290, San Jose, CA 95112.